The Un

Also by Anne Arnott

THE BRETHREN
JOURNEY INTO UNDERSTANDING
THE SECRET COUNTRY OF C. S. LEWIS
WIFE TO THE ARCHBISHOP
FRUITS OF THE EARTH

THE UNEXPECTED CALL

by

Anne Arnott

HODDER AND STOUGHTON
LONDON SYDNEY AUCKLAND
TORONTO

British Library Cataloguing in Publication Data
Arnott, Anne
The Unexpected Call

ISBN 0–340–2630 1

CONTENTS

Acknowledgments

I am grateful to Canon William Purcell, editor of *The Sign* magazine for permission to incorporate in this narrative extracts from a few short pieces which I wrote in that journal some years ago.

I also thank Mr. Bernard Palmer, editor of *The Church Times*, for permission to use part of my article, "Pilgrimage to Lindisfarne".

I am particularly glad that our son, the Reverend David Arnott, has been so willing for me to quote from his letters from Canada, in Chapter 7.

I cannot be too grateful to Mrs. Susan Toogood, without whose swift and expert typing this manuscript might never have been finished.

Above all, I have appreciated my husband's co-operation and advice in the telling of this narrative.

The woodcuts at the head of each chapter are by Thomas Bewick, the famous late eighteenth-century Tyneside engraver, and are taken from a few of the head and tail pieces to chapters in his "History of British Birds". Even today they still conjure up something of the flavour of Tyneside and Northumberland.

Anne Arnott
Levisham, 1981

Front cover and Reproductions by Kenneth Hitcham of Philipsons Studios, Newcastle upon Tyne.

Foreword

I have found myself gripped in reading this book. I am grateful for the honesty and courage with which the story is told, and not least for the humour which is never far from the surface.

The book has, I am sure, a word for many who ask what it means when a man says that he "has a call to the Ministry", particularly for those to whom the call comes in mid-life as it did to the husband of the author.

Equally it has something of importance and help to say to the wives and families of such men – and they are many – who find the whole tenor of their lives changed by what has happened to their husbands and their fathers. The depth of the change is not always fully appreciated – and it needs to be.

I have been moved by the writer's love of nature, of family, of fun, of society's outcasts, of the ministry, and of that Ministry's Lord. Reader, I think you will be, too.

Donald Coggan
Sissinghurst
Kent

Preface

What causes a successful professional man enjoying a satisfying career to give it up and take up a totally new life, facing the prospect of leaving home, friends and much work which is dear to him? My husband, a city solicitor, head of a family firm, did just this, and our lives were completely changed when he became an assistant curate in the Anglican church. We were questioned about this by many people, and were interviewed by the press and on radio and television. It was impossible then to give a quick answer, for the decision was a very difficult one, and only over the years did its full implication become apparent.

The story takes place mainly on Tyneside, to whose people we belong, and to whom we owe much. It is necessarily a personal account set down with great hesitancy and told just as it happened. In spite of an underlying serious purpose, it is far from being entirely solemn. Many humorous events have occurred, so that light and darkness have blended in an ever-merging pattern. If it gives encouragement to others, and there are many, who have also had an unexpected "call", then the writing of it will have been worthwhile.

At the request of the publisher, I have in Chapter 3, recapitulated briefly some of the events described in my first book, *The Brethren*, which is now out of print. This is for the greater clarification and understanding of the ensuing narrative.

1

Mission to a Corpse

The last night we spent on Tyneside, before leaving the home and countryside we loved, was distinctly macabre. In order to fulfil an unusual and long-standing promise to one of his clients, my husband had to undertake a mission to a corpse. It was to be his last act as a solicitor.

It was a summer evening as we drove south across the darkening moors of Northumberland and Durham. Heavy thunderclouds piling up from the west rolled massively across the brilliant red of a spectacular sunset. The empty desolate land stretched before us to an infinite distance in dimly undulating folds, occasionally gashed by a golden knife-thrust from the fast sinking sun, which was already partially obscured by the oncoming storm. We passed through the village of Blanchland with its low stone houses, almost golden in the evening light, clustered sleepily around the little square which was dominated by the ancient church where once a priory stood, and by the famous old inn, the Lord Crewe Arms. Then we came out onto bleak and desolate moorland country again, treeless for long stretches, and forbidding, until the road suddenly dropped sharply

down through the little town of Stanhope, which seems so
remote and stands like an outpost at the edge of the wild
country. Further on we went across the great Middleton
Common passing no one, until at last at dusk we saw the
land falling away to the River Tees in the valley far below.

It was nearly dark when we reached Romaldkirk, our
destination, a beautiful village on the border of North
Yorkshire, guarded by tall, majestic trees, with fine stone
houses around the green, and the fourteenth-century church
which still retains traces of Saxon work. When we stepped
out of the car into the scented night air, a few bats were
swooping and darting across the churchyard, a flutter of
little black shadows. The ancient tombstones, now barely
discernible, stood or leaned like silent watchers in the dim
light. It was very reminiscent of Gray's *Elegy*, and a feeling
of melancholy seemed to enfold the place, so that past
memories stirred gently and pressed around one like a
shroud.

The promise my husband had made years earlier to his
client, an elderly lady, was that he would see that the gold
cross on a chain she wore around her neck was on no account
removed at her death. Furthermore, in about the seventh
codicil to her will, she had bequeathed the ear-rings she
always wore to a relative. Now she had died, and her body
lay in its coffin in the church at Romaldkirk, awaiting the
funeral the next day.

Tom, my husband, had been away when she died, but
was dismayed on his return to find that the ear-rings had not
been removed as he had promised her. He is a man who
would not dream of betraying a trust, and so he had to act
fast. As no relatives were near he decided he must open the
coffin and remove them himself. It was rather a daunting
task. It was for this reason that we had driven fast and at a
late hour on this last night before we had to leave the north.
We had already been to our last evening service at our
church and to the gathering in the church hall afterwards
where many friends had come to say goodbye and to wish us
well.

At that hour we were not surprised to find the church locked. Tom disappeared in the darkness up a little path to some nearby cottages to discover where the caretaker lived. The tiny light of his torch appeared, bobbing up and down the garden paths as he went from one door to another, although he himself was lost to sight. Presently a faint wisp of light appeared inside the church, gently staining the windows as if candles had been placed by them, so soft and uncertain it seemed. A few minutes elapsed, and then I was aware of a figure beside me. Tom was back again, standing by the car, his face pale behind the light of the torch. "I'll need a screwdriver," he said, and opening the door, began to search rather distractedly among his tools. "Do you want to come into the church?" he added. But I was wrapped up in my own thoughts and, perhaps cowardly, did not want to enter the church with the body lying there. So I said "No," and at last he found what he wanted and vanished again. I did not envy him his task.

Time passed slowly, so I got out and walked to and fro, threading my way between the graves, and wondered about the corpse lying there so alone in the grey chill of the old church. In her lifetime, before her sight failed, she had been full of vitality. She had ridden her horse across the moors and fells, had loved the wild beauty of the country, and had watched the changing colours of those vast distances whose horizons are ever remote. She had been a character in her own way, respected by everyone in this place where she belonged. Now for her this life was over.

It seemed a long time later that I saw the lights in the church disappear, and I knew the mission must be accomplished. Tom reappeared, and we climbed quickly into the car. He revved up the engine and headed north again to Tyneside, to our home there for the last time. Rain started to fall heavily, splashing down the windscreen. We were cocooned in thick darkness except for the probing headlights sweeping ahead on the wet road. It was very late and we were tired and did not talk, until suddenly out of the blackness beside me I heard Tom say thoughtfully, "Her ear-lobes were very cold!"

Yes, cold she lay there, and in a strange way I felt a sort of kinship with her then. Just as her time to leave the land she loved had come, so too, in a quite different way, had ours, and I was cold at heart. Life as I knew it was ending; but if at that moment it seemed like a death, I had to believe that on the next day a new life would begin. Just then, like a birth, I found it painful.

2

The Call

Bright sunlight streaming into the window in the morning helped to dispel the sombre and apprehensive thoughts of the night before. We had to be up early to meet the removal men. The day promised to be chaotic. There was even a feeling of curiosity and excitement at the relentless turn of events. Now it was a matter of commitment. Faced with a totally new venture I knew we could never turn back.

The reason for this upheaval which had already altered our lives completely at a time when most of our friends had reached the apex of their careers, and when some were even beginning to think of taking things more easily, was, to put it plainly, a Call. It had come to Tom, and it had been drastic and unexpected. Once he tried to put something of what it meant to him in words.

"Sometimes there comes a moment in life when it feels as if God taps you on the shoulder and challenges you to leave your settled life, your home, your prosperity, and go out and do some special work for Him. It is agonising in a way to make your decision, to respond and take up the challenge.

There is so much to hold you back. Every thrust of reason and common sense checks you. Yet if you turned your back and refused to launch out into God's new way for you, your regret would be timeless. I think perhaps you could not live with yourself again." When he spoke like this, I could only respond inwardly, almost with numbness but, at heart, I knew that this was wholly true, and I must try as best I could to be ready for whatever happened. In any case, I had to admit it did cause an inward stir of excitement. Tom is a committed Christian. His faith is quiet and unflamboyant, but, as I had seen throughout our married life, it is steady and sure. He is generally a calm man who almost never needed to raise his voice to our lively family. They listened to him because he was reasonable and never fussed them. If quietly expressed, his love and affection for them were never in question. This made a secure background to their lives.

Yet, although outwardly he approached life with serenity, I always felt that since his days as a Lieutenant R.N.V.R. in the war, when he was in command of a minesweeping trawler, he inwardly chafed at the lack of physical adventure in his life. He had always enjoyed the spice of danger. A qualified master yachtsman, a horseman, a lover of remote and wild places, he had lived a full and interesting life. Later, while a leading professional man in the city of Newcastle upon Tyne, he had still found time for unexpected ventures, some of which figure in this story.

It was, however, in his Christian life that I felt he had wanted to be stretched. Certainly he served in many capacities. He was at one time national president of the Gideons, an international society of Christian business and professional men, known particularly for providing bibles for hotels, schools, hospitals, prisons and other places, putting them, as the American Gideons said, "in the traffic lanes of humanity". There were, indeed, many remarkable results of this rather unusual work. Not a few would-be suicides, alone in hotel bedrooms, had found new life from reading a Gideon bible; prisoners had received Christ as their Saviour while reading the New Testament in their cells; schoolchildren had begun to read the bible regularly. Tom also became a local lay reader in our home parish, and later a diocesan lay reader. Often he would travel many miles to take services in remote country parishes, sometimes for just a handful of people.

In his legal work he once said that he felt many of his clients really needed spiritual help at heart, which in his capacity it was not ethical to give. Too often, he said, he was just helping them to increase their incomes, but was not helping their true basic needs and problems. Perhaps, in the way one can sometimes see a pattern in life, as if an unseen hand is guiding you, it should not have been a surprise when an adventure of an unusual sort was suddenly offered him. While it did not at first appear dramatic, it became clear that it was an adventure of the spirit.

Tom was in his forties when he and certain other lay readers in the diocese of Newcastle were invited to consider joining a diocesan ordination school for mature laymen, to study for the ministry. There was a great shortage of ordained men, they were told. The need was becoming desperate. They were asked if they would consider giving some years before the normal age for retiring to serve God in the church. If so, they were told, they would be asked to give five years to work in the Newcastle diocese which covers much of Tyneside and all Northumberland, and to which area they all belonged.

Tom's forebears had belonged to Northumberland for generations, certainly since the beginning of the eighteenth century. Here he had grown up and belonged. It was his land, and he had a vast and specialised knowledge and understanding of it and its people. After much thought and prayer Tom gave his answer. He would take the course, and after this see if the way opened up for him to leave the family business in which he was the senior partner, provided full and proper arrangements could be made with his partners for the care of his clients. His partners would need to be willing to release him if he ultimately went ahead.

Tom now began four years of unremitting study in every

spare moment after full office hours. He attended evening lectures and wrote many lengthy essays. At the same time he carried on with all his normal legal work. Ultimately, when the way opened up, he spent a time at theological college. During these years the family seemed to see little of him. He was fascinated by and caught up with this study. Clearly a new world was opening up. "Dad's on a trip," our eldest son said. Certainly he was on a spiritual journey and it wholly gripped him.

It was a memorable day when Tom was finally ordained in Durham Cathedral by Bishop Ian Ramsey, a man little in stature but great in heart, brilliant in mind and loved by those who knew him and worked with him. Before then much was to happen, and our resolution was at times to be severely shaken, but we never envisaged leaving the north.

When the furniture was eventually stowed away by the late afternoon, and the removal men had arranged to meet us the next day in the south of England, we put the last cases in the car and locked the door of our home for the last time. It was not a moment I would care to repeat. As I turned away, the words of a friend at the farewell party the night before suddenly echoed in my mind and they have remained with me over the years. "Put us in a book one day," she said, "because that way you won't forget us." So, because this story belongs to those days on Tyneside, that is where the telling of it begins.

3

The Water of Tyne

Broad and dark and cold flowed the river far beneath the train in which I first crossed the High Level Bridge, and saw the other huge bridges spanning the Tyne. Just ahead lay Newcastle with its massive soot-blackened buildings and crowded jumble of houses jostling each other down to the quayside. It looked a stern, forbidding place, I thought, on that September evening; and as I left the train and stood under the huge, draughty portico of the station the air was sharp and cool. I was just twenty-two.

During my first weeks in the city I sometimes wondered what had driven me from the comforts of Bath where I had grown up, a place so architecturally beautiful, endowed with many parks and gardens, and gently sheltered by the surrounding hills. After university I had refused the chance of a good teaching post in the south of England. Work at that time was hard to get, and friends thought I was mad to turn it down. It was almost impossible to explain to them that I was searching for something. Nor did they understand the strange and compelling conviction which ultimately made me accept a post in a grammar school in Newcastle upon Tyne where the results of the great Depression still disastrously gripped the area.

As I sit by the fire during these dark winter evenings, I sometimes live over those days again, and see the city as I saw it then, with long, depressing streets of mean houses, and endless rows of slate roofs and chimneypots. Hopeless groups of unemployed men clustered round the street corners and children ran barefoot on the cold pavements. So the love affair that developed between me and the country beside the Tyne may seem surprising. It grew gradually as I learned to admire the people and to enjoy their shrewd, sturdy character, their courage and their refusal to be defeated. It came to embrace the whole county of Northumberland whose scenery is still, to me, some of the grandest and most exhilarating in the world. There was much I had to discover.

I shall not forget the moment when I first stood on Hadrian's Wall looking south from the Roman camp at Housesteads across the vast empty land which stretched beyond the point of vision into the furthest distance under the pale, clear, northern sky. Fresh winds blowing across the moors brought the scent of heather, and the curlews were calling with their wild, haunting cry. The very air seemed to pulse with life.

One day I went to Bamburgh where the massive castle stood majestically by the edge of the sea. Long, empty strands of silvery sand stretched beside it, and over the water I first saw Lindisfarne or Holy Island, which is surrounded by the sea for part of every day. I knew only the barest facts of its history then, as a great centre of early Celtic Christianity, but later I was to read everything I could find about it, wholly gripped by its story. It was to become a very special place to me.

A little further down the coast, at Embleton, I sat one summer evening on the high sand dunes as the harvest moon laid a brilliant path across the sea, and I listened to the echoing unearthly cry of the seals calling to each other, and sometimes a black head rose up out of the water, glistening in the silvery light.

There had been no money for luxuries in my life before, and the excitement was indescribable when I decided to spend regularly five precious shillings of my four pounds a week salary in learning to ride in the country just outside Newcastle. From the fields near Westerhope, where I first rode out, I could see on a clear summer evening the far northern Simonside hills, and great Cheviot slumbering in the misty, sunlit distance. Huge housing estates cover those fields now, but I can hear still the horses' thudding hooves, smell the may in full flower and feel the fresh breeze against my face.

Yet it was in the darkness of the city one night that I first realised why I had felt compelled to come to the North. One Saturday night, I was sitting in a bus that was rattling along the notorious Scotswood road towards Newcastle. I had been to see new friends in the country, and I remember the almost painful joy of walking in their large garden after weeks of being pent up in the city.

I left them in the late evening just as a storm of rain began. Now it was sluicing down the bus windows, washing down layers of dirt and dust in muddy rivulets. As we passed a broken gap in the long, dismal line of houses beside the road, many of whose windows were broken and stuffed with paper or rags, I saw several buildings which had just collapsed in an apparently forgotten mess of rubble. Through the space where they had stood a strong blast of wind burst through, shaking the bus and buffeting the windows. A sudden feeling of grief swept over me at the appearance of a poverty so total in this dismal area that nothing I had ever seen previously compared with it.

Inside the bus the air was stuffy and beer-laden. At each stop men and women emerged from the many pubs along the road and climbed rather unsteadily into the bus, shouting and smiling at each other. Some began to sing the Geordie's favourite song, "Blaydon Races". Its boisterous tune rose and fell rather uncertainly but the singing was full of a robust heartiness and enjoyment that belied the grimness of the singers' lives. I began to feel there was some quality in these people that just would not be defeated.

It was dark and still raining heavily when I got off the bus near Newcastle Central Station. As I walked through the wet streets I listened to the wind which was keening like a lament round the dirty houses and tenements. Paper lay in the gutters and blew across the pavements. Half-hidden figures huddled in doorways, sometimes clasped together as if to wrench comfort and warmth out of the desolate surroundings.

Suddenly I saw a little group of people coming towards me. They were momentarily illumined by the light of a street lamp. Striding briskly out of the shadows into the driving rain which slanted across the arc of light, came the priest from St. John's Church in the dark heart of the city. His long cassock swung as he walked, and his black cloak flew out behind him in the rising wind. The black shovel hat, glistening with raindrops, framed a face that shone with a kind of inner joy and merriment. On each side of him, leaping and jumping in and out of the puddles, bare feet splashing up and down, were two tiny, ragged boys holding him by the hand, and their eyes sparkled and danced in their thin, dirty little faces. They were all three laughing together, oblivious of the darkness around them, and for a moment there seemed a radiance about them that reached out and touched the watcher with the warmth of sunshine in that dismal street.

I knew then why I had come to the far north of England. I was looking for God. I believed it was in the dark places where He so often might be found, and now I had seen a reflection of His Spirit in the face of a man who was a complete stranger.

I had felt very much alone that night in the depressing streets of Newcastle. I had come to the city young and very inexperienced, but eager to see real life, about much of which I was totally ignorant. Although I had lived to the full at London University, I had previously led a very sheltered life, for a peculiar barrier existed between my puritan home and the fascinating world outside. It was a little like living in a fortress. One could peer through the windows at passers-by in the street, even wave to them sometimes, but they remained distant, apart from our life within. Inside, my home was comfortingly secure, loving, warm, intellectually academic – and separate. Books were crammed into every room, overflowing on to tables and chairs. I learned about life from reading them avidly. On the whole I was happy, assured of my parents' affectionate care at all times, and only gradually did I realise that other people's homes were quite different. By then I was not particularly interested. I was safe and content where I was, except at those times when it was secretly very painful to feel I was somehow different from my school friends.

I was a "meeting child", brought up among the Plymouth Brethren, now generally known as the Open or Christian Brethren, of whom my doctor father was a loyal and convinced member. It is necessary to state clearly that he never belonged to the secretive and exclusive group whose misguided activities still often lead to the tragic break-up of families. This has even received publicity in the press, where the title Plymouth Brethren is often wrongly applied to them.

The Brethren among whom I grew up, however, formed a Biblically-based open fellowship, who met very simply, rather in the manner of the Society of Friends, in halls and meeting-rooms Sunday by Sunday, to "remember the Lord in the breaking of Bread". As they saw it, their gathering was as close as possible to the apostolic pattern of the early church, described by Luke in the Book of Acts. There was no priest or minister. Different brethren, never "sisters", spoke "as they were led", reading from the Bible and expounding the passage. Prayers were offered, and these were often long and always extempore. Ever restless, I disgraced myself more than once by wriggling so much on the hard, polished wooden seat, that I fell off it on to my head on the floor, causing quite a disturbance.

A few hymns were always sung from a sober book considered doctrinally sound called *Hymns of Light and Love*. These were very solemn and devotional, but, to me as a lively child, not inspiring. They were sung unaccompanied, for the large harmonium which stood on the little platform was not used on Sunday mornings, as this might distract the weaker spirits, I was given to understand. Clearly, I was one of these, for I longed for lively rhythms and stirring, uplifting music. Yet I had to admit that the voices of "the saints" – as the Brethren alluded to each other in St. Paul's words describing believers – often rose and fell in a strange sweet harmony, which was surprising, because when the elder brother responsible for raising the tune uttered his first clarion notes, we never knew exactly how we were going to take off. Then, as first one and then another of the stronger voices joined in, we followed the lead and suddenly the notes blended together. Only in Wester Ross in a small mission hut beside a tiny, remote bay, have I heard the same sort of spontaneous harmony, and there it mingled with the cry of the seagulls flying to and fro outside, and the wind seemed to echo and take up the sound; and there was a longing and a yearning in the melody of voices as the "Wee Frees" sang their solemn praises from the Psalms.

Although I often longed to escape from the meeting, out of the gospel hall into the sunlight of the shabby back street where it was situated, I grew slowly to accept the discipline of that quiet Sunday morning hour and a half. A wise Quaker, a senior sister in a large hospital, once told me to my interest that this time of quiet was most beneficial to the health and well-being of very lively children. Today, I suppose, transcendental meditation and yoga have stressed the value of stillness and peace but, as far as I am concerned, they lack the "soul comfort" which I learned in those early days which seem so vivid but so long ago. For whatever the worship may have lacked in outward beauty of surroundings, or liturgical beauty of language, was largely compensated by the total sincerity and deep devotion to their Lord of those who gathered in humility in that plain place to worship so simply and quietly.

Even when I was quite young I had a deep admiration for my father, and regarded his complete dedication to Christ with awe. I knew he was a leading physician in Bath, distinguished by remarkable success in his work. This was no surprise to me. I saw him often enough at his prayers, and I knew he committed everything he did, every patient, every difficult case, to Christ. Yet he was very human. His deep, unwavering faith was coupled with great vitality, and real zest for life. He had an intense interest not only in people but in nature, in every bird and beast. He also had a vivid and sometimes unexpected sense of humour, when some funny event would leave him helpless with laughter, with tears running down his cheeks.

My mother, a London vicar's daughter, was an academic, a brilliant mathematician, who had been an early student at Royal Holloway College, later to become part of London University. She became a teacher in notable schools, ending up at the remarkably young age of twenty-nine, as headmistress of the Royal School for army officers' daughters at Bath. Here she met my father, then the school medical officer, a widower with two teenage daughters. To everyone's surprise, and I think to hers, she married him during the First World War. She was, and remained, devoted to him. In attempting to unite a difficult and divided family – although this failed, for my older sisters were totally out of sympathy with my father's way of worship and puritan life – she left the Anglican church, to which I believe she remained wholly loyal at heart, and joined my father's meeting. I think this cost her a great deal, but she hid it all in the privacy of her own heart. She was really a happy person, lively and interested in everything. She had a very human side, often suggesting and carrying out "little treats", to enliven our days. These were generally simple in the extreme, and she and I might set off together to ride on top of a tram to the outskirts of the city, and have tea in a tea-garden. On really great days we took the bus to Bristol to go to the zoo. Occasionally we even went by train to London to see the sights. At home she loved to relax with a good novel, and wherever we went one was tucked into her bag. Like my father, she had a great sense of humour and could skilfully mimic pompous and fussy people, and we would laugh happily together at the foibles of mankind. She was always so full of ideas and was so stimulating that she made my little world seem far bigger and more exciting than it actually was.

The Bible was, of course, my parents' charter for life. Every morning for about an hour before it was time to get up at seven o'clock, my father, wrapped in a warm brown dressing-gown, and even wearing gloves in very cold winter weather, sat and studied it in his little cold dressing-room before beginning his day. He would read the Scriptures in both Hebrew and Greek, in both of which he was self-taught. When the family had assembled for breakfast at eight o'clock, he took family prayers every day, reading a short passage of the Bible aloud in his strong, melodious voice, while the three maids sat solemn, poker-faced, in a row in front of the ornately-carved antique sideboard. The music of the words rose and fell, and the sound washed over me like the echo of distant seas on a far-off shore, haunting, never to be forgotten.

My mother, an eternal student at heart, had a deep interest in biblical archaeology. She did much research, and made a number of trips to the British Museum, when she usually took me with her. She wrote learned papers on the subject, which were ultimately published in some journals abroad.

Although happily I had two or three special friends, I grew up a solitary child for the most part, for my older sisters had left home by the time I was at the High School. Yet I grew to realise that I lived with two remarkable and loving people who were often fun to be with, and courageous and steadfast in their faith. They both had a strong social concern for the poor and the sick, to whom my father devoted his busy life, and in that respect at least I was taught to be outward-looking. My father ran a medical mission every Wednesday in a very poor area of Bath, to give free help and treatment to those who could not afford it in those days before the National Health Service.

When eventually I left home at the age of eighteen, I went, like my mother and one of my sisters, to London University, and, to me, a dazzling and totally new life. It spelled excitement, freedom, sport, pleasures such as I had never tasted before in my unworldly home, and friends of every outlook. I had inherited something of great value from my parents, an unbreakable zest for life.

A more serious realisation grew steadily in my mind at this time, that I could not for ever have a second-hand faith, basking in the warmth and security of my parents' firm and reassuring beliefs. Some time I must find a valid faith of my own. I had one great advantage: having seen Christianity so powerfully and consistently lived out in their lives, I knew without a shadow of doubt that it really worked. They meant business, as someone once said to me. They had taken Christ's words to Peter literally: "Launch out into the deep." They had not remained in shallow waters, but I was still on the edge, hesitant, afraid, although I knew all the answers.

How often at the evangelistic gospel meetings in our hall on Sunday evenings, had I heard the constant appeal to give one's heart to the Lord. Often this had been alarmingly expressed. It was suggested that sudden death might overtake one, and one would die in one's sins, unsaved. Or else, we were told, the Second Coming of our Lord to earth to gather up his saints was imminent. It might well take place that very night and if we were not converted, not truly committed Christians, we would be left behind. After such exhortations, and the fervent singing of hymns from a much more dramatic hymn book with red floppy covers, called *Redemption Songs and Solos*, I prayed earnestly night after night to be saved, and to become a true child of God. I do not think my parents, essentially kind, really approved of these battering-ram methods of evangelism. However, there were other, more gifted and eloquent speakers who had a

genuine and moving sincerity, and a true and loving passion
for souls that was far more impressive. I always listened to
them intently. But the questions remained, and I longed for
assurance.

Such feelings rather vanished during university days.
Religion grew to be a more natural part of life. Faith was far
less pressurised and strained. I found a niche by becoming
the social secretary of the Student Christian Movement.
Deeply concerned at the problems of unemployment which
were more devastating in certain areas even than now, for
many families faced near-starvation, I studied many books
on social work. On Sundays and on each weekday morning
I sang in chapel in the college choir, and the beauty of the
services which meant little or nothing to some people, were
an inspiration to me. Amidst all the heady excitement of
those days I knew at heart that after taking my degree I
wanted to work for God in some way. I believed quite
simply that I should be told where to go.

In my finals year my father dashed out, in the middle of
one night, to see a dying friend, whose young doctor had
refused to turn out. On his return he collapsed unconscious
on the floor. He had had a severe stroke and became a
bedridden invalid for a year. I found it tragic, for he had
been ceaselessly active.

It was now a vital necessity that I should get a good
teaching post at once. My parents faced great poverty. It
was after applying for many jobs that I saw a post in
Newcastle upon Tyne advertised in the *Times Educational
Supplement*. The words stood out. I had the strongest and
strangest conviction that that was the place where I was
meant to go. I knew no one in Newcastle and I had never
been there. It was frontier country to me, and in those days
seemed as far from the sophisticated Georgian city of Bath
as Katmandu is from Britain.

When I was offered the post, I knew with certainty that
God *was* directing me. My journey into faith had begun.

I had only been two months in Newcastle on the night
when I walked through its dark streets and saw the unknown

priest, whose face was alight with a kind of inner joy, and the two small boys who must have come from the notorious slums of the west end. It was one of those inexplicable moments that stand out, and the mind is illuminated as if with a sudden shaft of sunlight. Words of Jesus from the gospel of St. John floated through my mind: "If a man love me, he will keep my words: and my Father will love him, and we will come unto him, and make our abode with him."

I had wanted reality and assurance. Now I saw that when we cannot *feel* Christ's presence in our lives, we can actually see Him in the lives of others in whom his Holy Spirit truly lives. It is a solemn and beautiful recognition. At that moment I had experienced it in the loneliness and the darkness, and like Thomas the doubter I could say, "My Lord, and my God."

I felt then that it was freedom in life, not shackles, which was being offered. I chose freedom.

A few weeks after the night when I had walked alone through the dark streets of Newcastle, I found myself one Sunday morning in the upper room of a gaunt, stone building known as the old schools, which stood above the broad, cold River Tyne at Wylam, a large residential village with many pleasant houses set in gardens not far from the city centre of Newcastle. The room was bare and plain, and had hard, wooden benches and chairs set in a square around a small table covered with spotless linen cloth, on which stood a glass goblet of wine and a crusty loaf on a plate. This was the meeting-place of a small gathering of the Brethren, where an elderly doctor ruled over "the saints" with vigour and what I can only describe as panache. He was a great character, strong and dynamic in life, and would have reminded me forcibly of a pugilist, so square and heavy was his jaw and so determined the set of his mouth, had it not been for the hint of nobility in the aquiline nose, and the fierce good humour that glinted from kindly eyes, which bore witness to a broad humanity. He and his elderly sister, equally as dominating a character, were a formidable but very kindly pair, and were friends of my father. They had invited me to spend Sunday with them.

I had not really intended to go back to a Brethren meeting after I left home. I went to churches of various denominations on Tyneside, trying to find one to whose fellowship I could whole-heartedly belong. Some seemed disappointingly lifeless – even dead; others, in particular a lively Presbyterian church, were friendly and stimulating and I felt happy to go there.

I had felt at that time that I could not agree to all the Brethren's man-made rules of conduct. I had been given a conscience. I needed freedom to use it. The guiding reins had been held too tightly. I did not feel it right for any human to control or dictate my actions. I believed God would guide and direct one's life. I felt that, while the Brethren stressed Pauline doctrines and Old Testament truths, with the exception of the Crucifixion they did not stress the gospel narratives enough, and this seemed to me deficient, because I wanted to study and consider all that the life of Jesus implied. So when the doctor kindly invited me out to spend the day I was uneasy. Yet I knew I would receive nothing but kindness from this unusual couple.

When I arrived I was given an enthusiastic welcome. This, in my experience, was common in all Brethren meetings. The warm, inner fellowship could be deeply comforting to the lonely and insecure, and to those for whom it was the right place to be. It was when one could not wholly subscribe to the Brethren's methods and practice that one was in real trouble, because to them their way was bibilically, infallibly right. All the sects were unsound in some particular, they maintained. The simple apostolic practice of meeting to break bread and to remember the Lord had been overlaid, they claimed, with many and various man-made rituals. At times I almost agreed with them; but I believed from Christ's teaching that it was above all else the *spirit* in which one worshipped God that was far more important than different methods of administration, which could depend on tradition and upbringing and much else. The Scriptures were clear about this: "There are differences of administration but the same Lord," Paul declares. So I sat a little uneasily – and yet gratefully too – in that small gathering of devout people.

Suddenly I looked up and became aware that an interesting and distinguished-looking family had quietly entered, and were sitting opposite. An elderly man, who had the air of a retired army officer, sat with his Bible open on his knee. He had a look of quiet serenity. By him sat a beautiful young woman – I was aware of her striking dark eyes – and by her a tall young man with a peaceful expression. He had a strong face, and I had the impression that he was looking far away at distant horizons beyond the confines of the little upper room. So it came about that I saw Tom for the first time.

My first feeling was that I had never before seen such interesting people in any of the meetings I had been to. Did this family really fit into the little fellowship, I wondered. Did they have no doubts? Did they subscribe to the same puritan way of life in which I had grown up, I wondered. I had, for example, never been to a theatre or cinema before I went to university, which my friends found inexplicable and eccentric. For the time being all my questions remained unanswered. The doctor and his sister told me a little more however. Tom was a solicitor, as was his father. His sister looked after their home further west up the Tyne as their beautiful mother had tragically died when they were tiny children. She also studied music in Newcastle.

Early in the new year Tom's sister invited me out to spend one Saturday at their home. It was a very cold day, and we were standing in the attractive kitchen by a cosy, flickering fire while outside a red-gold sunset was casting its light over the gardens and fields beyond. It had been a happy day because we were finding we laughed at the same things, and could share various experiences. Suddenly the door opened and Tom appeared there quite unexpectedly. He had been riding and I thought he looked impressive in his jacket and breeches. At that moment everything about him seemed to fit into the character of the cold, beautiful Northumbrian landscape, which slowly but surely was weaving a spell over me and captivating my imagination.

As we talked over tea, I found I was increasingly intrigued by this courteous, kind family who, it appeared, were interested in so many fascinating activities: sailing, canoeing, riding, and much else.

That night Tom drove me back to my digs in Newcastle in his little M.G. sports car. I lived in a long, rather gloomy street of terraced houses in the west end of the city. My life and his seemed worlds apart. I found him quietly impressive as he talked, for he had a fund of knowledge about an extraordinary variety of odd subjects. He began to talk about bees which he kept at Barnard Castle, forty miles to the south, where he was working at that time. I knew virtually nothing about bees and felt very ignorant. That subject would not get us far, I suspected. I had a feeling he would not be easy to get to know, for he seemed reserved and quietly self-sufficient. I was still learning about bees when we said goodbye at the dark front door.

As I thought over the day, I realised that it was wonderful to have been able to relax into an atmosphere of mutual understanding, with nothing hidden, nothing to be concealed or misunderstood, because Tom and his sister's home was like my own. We had the same unusual background that so many people just could not understand. One thing was very clear. Tom and his sister had a quiet true Christian faith, and there was both serenity and merriment in their attitude to life.

As the months went on I saw Tom very rarely indeed. One day he was at his home when I was there and we went out for a walk together. We did not talk very much. Life was so uncertain, for the spectre of war was drawing relentlessly closer. Gas masks were handed out and trenches dug in the Newcastle streets. To be young then was to live for the moment, savouring every joy, every excitement with a deep, intense awareness, knowing that we might be on the brink of a terrible holocaust, and that there might be no future for us at all.

During the long hot tense summer of 1939, I went out riding whenever I could afford it. Tom's sister came to ride with me one Saturday at Westerhope, just outside Newcastle. A week or two later I went alone to the riding-school one restless May evening when the land was golden in the evening sunlight, and rode out with Danny, the loquacious riding-master, and a few other people. Danny drew his horse level with mine at one point and said, "So you know Miss Arnott. She rides well. But you should see her brother. He's a very fine horseman, for sure." I turned quickly away, looking at the distant blue Cheviot hills. "Really," I said lightly, "that's interesting."

We cantered back into the stable yard later, I reined in my chestnut mare and suddenly saw a small M.G. sports car. No, surely it could not be. Tom was forty miles away. I dismounted, and was in time to see Danny's jaw drop as Tom came forward. "I thought we might go out to supper," he said. "They told me at your digs where you were." I could not believe it. Tom was so cool and off-hand. Why had he bothered to come and search me out?

"Well, you silenced Danny," I said later. "He was talking about you, and I never let on I even knew you."

We had supper in a large pub near Westerhope. I learned that Tom was very busy as commandant of the Auxiliary Fire Service at Barnard Castle. He hoped eventually to be called up and go into the Navy, and to serve on mine-sweepers. "I could never kill," he said. "I only want to save life. But we must fight this fearful oppression under Hitler."

"If war breaks out, we are being evacuated with the children to some secret destination in Cumberland, I believe," I said rather bleakly. I did not know when or if I would see Tom again.

Just before war was declared the school where I taught was evacuated to Wigton near Carlisle. We had to become parents, teachers, sisters, all rolled into one, to the children taken from their parents and put so often into totally unsuitable billets where they were not wanted. Thousands of children had marched to Newcastle station that day, with gas masks and a day's ration of food, and as train after train drew out, Newcastle became like a city of the dead, all the children gone and only grieving parents left behind. That evacuation only lasted two terms for the "phoney war", as it was called, lulled people into a sense of false security. We trekked back to Newcastle thankfully to start work normally in our own school for the summer term of 1940.

During those days I was invited to spend a weekend in a farmhouse near Warcop in Cumbria with Tom's family. We walked together among the high fells and beside the beautiful and gentle River Eden. It was a wonderful weekend but again we did not know when or if we would meet again. Tom was called up shortly afterwards, and soon became an able seaman on the aircraft carrier *Victorious*, and virtually vanished. France fell. The tremendous drama of Dunkirk took place, and we listened breathless to Churchill's matchless words on our radio sets.

Our school was swiftly re-evacuated, and this time our train drew out of Newcastle with fighter aircraft to escort us. We found ourselves at Ambleside in the Lake District, strangely remote and cut off from the world where we belonged. The days dragged on. We endured a winter more severe than anything I had ever experienced. Snow lay feet deep. The mountains glistened and shone, all harsh outlines blurred. We climbed one by moonlight, hearing only the cry of an owl as we ascended the steep, silvery slopes, and sheep bleating in a distant farm far below. We reached the top ridge at last and stood in a cold, remote, lunar world of unearthly beauty.

As the months passed I heard from Tom occasionally. The *Victorious*, we heard on the news, had been involved in the great chase of the *Bismark*. Then there was no letter for weeks.

Meanwhile my father had made an almost miraculous recovery from his serious illness. He had had to give up his practice, but had been asked to go back as consultant physician to the Bath and Wessex Orthopaedic Hospital because so many of the doctors had been called up. He loved this post and was able, to his delight, to do much work for children again. But he and my mother were not strong. They had left our beautiful Georgian home in the Circus and had rented a much smaller, quite attractive stone house. Sadly I felt they needed me at home. I applied for and got a post in a large boys' grammar school in Bath, as a number of the masters had joined the forces. I had been three years in the North. Now I found I missed it intolerably. Surprisingly, it had become my country. Only later I learned that my mother's parents and forebears came from the borders near Carlisle and Newcastle. It was strange.

One September day Tom suddenly arrived at my home in Bath. He had been one of the men chosen to train as an officer. I found I was overjoyed to see him again and quite surprised, but it was very difficult to say all the things we wanted. The times were so uncertain. We had met so little, really. Shortly before he left to go home to Northumberland, I was preparing a meal in the kitchen. Tom walked in and quite suddenly asked me to marry him. At first I could hardly believe it. But at that moment the fragmented bits of my life suddenly fused into one. Tom, I knew, was the only person who could reconcile my worlds, and I had come to feel that life without him would be sad and empty.

We were married in February, six months later, in the Brethren's meeting-hall, chiefly for my father's sake as it became clear that to have the wedding anywhere else would have greatly distressed him. Tom was now a sub-lieutenant, R.N.V.R.

In bitter weather we set off by train for a fortnight's honeymoon in the picturesque Cornish fishing village of Polperro. Four days later Tom was recalled to Whale Island, near Portsmouth, to do further immediate training. Our honeymoon was untimely over. I went sadly back to my job until the end of term. Then, with many good wishes from all the masters among whom I had grown to feel happy, and who had mercilessly teased me and the other few women in the staff-room, which had all made for a good time during difficult days, I left. I was touched when a number of the boys brought me small presents they had made themselves – a tiny model Spitfire made as a brooch, and much else. "Every nice girl loves a sailor", the fifth form had sung with great good humour when I got married. Being there had, after all, been a good experience.

I took a train to Edinburgh, an adventure in itself in those troubled days, and joined Tom in a tiny hotel in Queensferry. It was full of officers' wives, waiting for their husbands' ships, and never knowing what the day would hold. Many had lost homes in the blitz on the large cities during the previous two years, and now simply followed the fleet, living a half life wherever they could, picking up jobs, or taking children with them. At last Tom was posted to Tilbury Docks, to join a flotilla of mine-sweepers. He found digs at Gravesend, just across the river near the ferry, where he could come when off duty. I found a job teaching in a school at Greenhithe. Half of it had been blasted to bits by bombs. We taught in what was left. Air-raid sirens were constantly going off, although for the time being the heaviest raids had ceased.

It was during this period, when Tom was going up and down the English Channel in very dangerous waters, that a strangely dirty envelope in my mother's handwriting arrived by post. The very brief note inside told me that my home in Bath had been destroyed the night before in a very heavy air-raid, and my father had been slightly wounded in the head, but my parents, who had sheltered under the stairs, were quite miraculously alive, and safe for that one night in a hospital up the road. They had lost everything. The news was shattering. I then heard on the radio just after receiving the letter that another heavy air-raid on Bath had taken place the next night. I tried to phone – but where? Telephone communication with Bath had, it seemed, simply ceased. I was heartbroken for my brave father and mother, whose steady faith had always touched and inspired me. There had been no word of lament or horror in the letter, simply a quiet acceptance of anything that the Lord might permit. Now I could not get in touch with them at all. Perhaps they had been killed in the second raid. I felt frantic. I did not even know where they were.

Tom's senior officer most kindly sent him off immediately on compassionate leave and we took the train to Bath to find them. In fact the train could not get to Bath. The station was smashed. We stopped some miles outside and buses took us into the city, where the chaos, the rubble, the wrecked buildings, the glass-filled roads, all presented a terrible sight.

After searching the duplicated lists of the many dead which were posted at various places, and not finding my parents' names, we began trying to contact people who might know where they were. At last, to my great joy, we found a phone that actually worked, and discovered they were living in the attics of elderly friends on the outskirts of Bath. Our reunion was traumatic, redeemed by my mother's comic appearance in a variety of odd garments kind folk had given her. She had been in her nightdress at the time of the raid, and had lost all her clothes. The memory of my father's serenity has remained with me to this day. No anger, no moaning at a cruel fate, simply the quiet words: "During the raid I held mother's hand, and we said the Lord's prayer together, and we felt we were not alone." Never then, nor at any time after, did he complain at what had happened. They lived in the attic bedroom, cared for by the friends, for two years. Tramping the city each day in total weariness, my mother could find no house or flat available within their means, for so many thousands of houses had been destroyed. At last, towards the end of the war, a rather shabby maisonette was found to rent, and they moved into it for the last years of life, physically shaken by the violent turn of events, but with their faith undimmed. One great joy came to them. It was the birth of two small grandsons, and then later a little grand-daughter.

Tom was stationed at Aberdeen when David was born towards the end of the war. Partly through anxiety, I think, at the impending second front to which Tom expected to go, I became very ill indeed, alone in a tiny attic flatlet while he was at sea. I had to have an emergency Caesarean section operation, and David, given a fifty per cent chance of survival, was a month premature and weighed just over four pounds. Somehow I was sure he would live, and when at last I took him home to the attic, my parents made the great pilgrimage to see the tiny baby. In our little sitting-room in the flat, we had a simple service dedicating him to God, attended by kind friends from a large and unusually lively meeting we often went to, although we frequently went to the Church of Scotland also. We asked in faith that he might be a good soldier of Jesus Christ, and my father read some beautiful words from the Psalms.

Soon afterwards we were turned out of the attic flat summarily. The owners did not want a baby in the house. I pushed the pram through the streets of Aberdeen, searching day after day for lodgings, getting more and more weary, and praying desperately for a home. I had visited forty houses, when the answer came that I had looked for. A lady with two small children, and a husband missing in Singapore, worked as a school matron, and could let us have her little bungalow outside Aberdeen during term-time. We were reprieved. It was like a miracle. David grew and prospered, a lively, intelligent and alert little baby.

The relief when war ended cannot be described. Tom went down to Barnard Castle and found a small semi-detached house ruined by damp, for all the pipes had burst one winter, during the owners' absence. It was going very cheap, had good potential, and we could dry it out and decorate it. It was the only house we could afford, and to us it was quite wonderful to have a home of our own. My happiness was indescribable. The nightmare years were over. We could begin to live again. We now attended a lively Methodist church. Tom was active in the church, and was put "on the plan" often taking services, and even preaching in a large open-air service in the market place.

Three years later Chris was born, a happy, healthy little

boy with a strong look of Tom about him. David, by now, was endlessly adventurous, and often accident-prone. One needed eyes in the back of one's head if he was to be prevented from fearful mishaps as he climbed everywhere, curious to see and examine everything.

When Chris was a year old, Tom had to decide what to do about the family practice in Newcastle. His father's age and health meant that he would have to take over the practice if it was to continue. Schools there were good, and perhaps it was right that we should return. We had been very happy in Barnard Castle, but I was still drawn to Northumberland. We discussed it from all angles. Tom was regretful. He loved his life in Barnard Castle, and had many contacts all around the countryside. But he was the fourth solicitor in succession in his family, and was unwilling to let the Newcastle connection go. At last he decided we must return north to the city.

And what of our faith during these years? I do not think in times of great anxiety or danger it is right or necessary to be constantly introspective or self-questioning. It is a time for simply holding on to one's deep belief that, come what may, Christ will be with those who call on Him, in the darkness, in the despair, as well as in the joys. This was how I felt but, by nature extrovert, and always fascinated by all aspects of natural life, I always had a core of happiness. Even on the worst days the sun had shone at times, and the words of George Borrow in *Lavengro* seemed not inappropriate to describe one's feelings: "There's night and day, brother, both sweet things; sun, moon, and stars, brother, all sweet things; there's likewise a wind on the heath. Life is very sweet, brother; who would wish to die?"

So we went back to live by the water of Tyne, and did not then know that this decision was momentous, and that eventually much more would be asked of us.

4

First Encounter

We returned with our two small boys, David and Christopher, to live three miles from the centre of Newcastle in an urban area. Here our daughter Cathy was born. These were years when Tom was working exceedingly hard to build up and expand the city practice, and he also opened two branch offices in rural areas of Northumberland. During this time my parents died within a year of each other, leaving, at first, a gap that I felt would never be filled. Yet I had many happy and unforgettable memories of them.

Running a house and looking after the children filled my days, and after the terrible strains and traumas of the war, the immediate post-war years were a merciful release from stress. I was, I think, simply content to *be*, not questioning anything, but absorbing the joy of knowing that a day might be filled with ordinary, undramatic, even trivial events. To be peacefully at home with the family was real joy.

At first it was very convenient to live so close to the city and to good schools, but we always felt that we should really like to live further out and nearer the country. When the children were in bed, I sometimes used to cycle out on summer evenings to gaze at likely houses for sale. It became quite a hobby, but somehow none of them ever seemed quite right. "It hasn't the right feel," I would report. I scanned the advertisements in the local papers and visited various pretentious houses for "business executives", but in the end began to feel that the house we wanted did not exist.

We had lived on the outskirts of the city for six years, when quite by chance one day my eye fell on a small, very unobtrusive advertisement in small print, of a family house for sale at Ryton on the southern side of the Tyne, eight miles west of Newcastle. Tom and I went together to see over it. When we walked up the stone steps to the front door and stepped into the long, light hall and saw glimpses of a sunlit garden through a conservatory door at the end of it, we both felt at home, and knew suddenly and instinctively that we had found the right place. We were shown all over the house. "This is a happy place," I said to Tom, but even I was surprised at the speed with which he made an immediate offer for it, which was accepted. It was not, in fact, a fashionable house, nor was it in a fashionable area, but it was a house of character, over one hundred years old, and we loved it from the first.

Ryton, where we now went to live, had originally been a picturesque village standing on a hill above the River Tyne. The houses clustered around the village green near the beautiful thirteenth-century parish church of the Holy Cross, whose very unusual, lead-covered spire rose 120 feet high, a landmark for miles around. At least one rector of Ryton had become Archbishop of Canterbury, and the church had many features of historical interest. Beside it one of the finest rectories in the country, from an architectural point of view, stood in spacious gardens. It was a large, stone mansion, part of whose interior dated from Elizabethan times, although the imposing stone façade was built in the days of Queen Anne. On the village green outside the rectory gates stood the remains of a stone cross where John Wesley had once preached.

Over the years the Industrial Revolution had engulfed

Ryton. Five collieries surrounded it, and rows of miners' houses grew up in the vicinity. By the time we went there the pits had begun to close down, and the character of Ryton was changing. New estates, both of council and private houses, had sprung up around the old village. Often old and new houses jostled together, surprisingly harmoniously. To the east, new factories were being built, and away down the hill towards Newcastle the view was massively industrial, where the four huge cooling towers of Stella Power Station stood sentinel beside the Tyne. Yet something of the village atmosphere still lingered on. The open country of Northumberland lay just across the county boundary about three miles to the west of our home, and a short walk down the hill from the old village led through leafy woods to the Willows, a long stretch of riverside common, a favourite place for walks, where children played, and often at weekends many people made their way there to watch the dinghies of the yacht club sailing on the broad reaches of the river.

Our house stood in a road full of architectural variety. There were houses of every type, old and new, Victorian terraced, detached Victorian, as well as modern detached houses and bungalows, and surprisingly they all blended quite happily together. There was even a stone farmhouse a little lower down the road from us, whose fields stretched away westwards.

Moorside itself was only two storeys high, being long and sturdy, built largely of stone with some brick facings. Stone steps led from the front garden to the stone-pillared porch. Inside, the rooms opening off the hall were spacious. There was a broad staircase leading to the four main bedrooms and, to the delight of the family, a back staircase led out of the large farmhouse-type kitchen to two more bedrooms where in past decades the servants slept. There was even a cellar, into whose dark depths the children gleefully led their envious friends down rather precipitous stone stairs. It was, in short, totally un-labour saving and old-fashioned, but it was a real home. The pleasant enclosed garden at the back had a big lawn, and here the family became croquet fiends. There was an ancient green and white summerhouse which perpetually and drunkenly leaned to the south, and whose door would never shut properly. The children played many games in it, and once turned it into a museum full of curious treasures.

From the moment we arrived, I had the feeling that the house welcomed us and accepted us unreservedly, almost as if it had been waiting for our arrival. As the months passed, I felt in it an atmosphere of peace and permanence. It seemed to shelter and protect us, and welcome us back when we had been away. Fanciful as this may be, there is no doubt that certain houses do have a special atmosphere. Our daughter once said thoughtfully that a certain beautiful and ancient church felt as if "its stones were soaked in prayer". Similarly, houses which have been lived in and loved by happy and good people seem to impart something of the emotions that have been felt and expressed within them, just as if the very bricks and stones absorbed the spirit of the occupants, which I am inclined to believe they do.

The days at Moorside were full and happy. The boys went off each day by bus to the Royal Grammar School in Newcastle, and Tom also travelled into the city to his office each day. Cathy, only three years old when we went there, played happily about the house and garden, or tried helping to cook, standing on a stool beside the large kitchen table, and learning to make pastry. Her favourite ploy was to squeeze and roll little lumps of dough until they became grey and glutinous. She played with our various animals who lived at different times with us, Storm the magnificent Newfoundland dog, the various cats, their many kittens, the mice which so disastrously escaped from time to time, Bruce and Bonny the Border terriers, and Chris's pet grass snakes which also escaped once, causing a neighbour to have near hysterics when one slithered at top speed into her front hall. Later Cathy went to school in Newcastle too.

As I look back, Moorside seems full of sunlight. Like all

families we had our difficult and anxious times, but on the whole our life there was very happy. On a deeper level there was another reason why it was a significant time. The search for God, which years earlier had for me been linked with my decision to teach in the north of England before the war, was to take on a new depth and direction. It was almost as if one was slowly awakening to hear new sounds, new voices. There was the feeling that just possibly something exciting might be about to happen. I had, of course, no idea at first what it might be, nor that these years were to become a time of challenge and that this would be due in no small measure to our encounter with a remarkable man.

When we went to Ryton we wanted to find a church that was really alive, whose fellowship we could join, particularly for the sake of the children. We wanted them to find a joyful and sustaining faith of their own as they grew up. I remained totally convinced that this alone was the basis of true happiness.

Although Tom and I had joined in the worship of a variety of churches, chapels and meetings over the years, we now wanted to find one to which we could wholeheartedly belong, and perhaps make some contribution to its life, if that was possible. We wanted it to be somewhere that was a happy place for the children, too.

When we came to Ryton we heard some talk about a new vicar at Newburn, just across the river, a decayed industrial area, outwardly an unpromising place. It appeared that people were travelling for miles to the parish church to hear his inspirational preaching. On our first Sunday at Ryton, perhaps out of curiosity, Tom took David and Chris across the bridge over the Tyne to Newburn. They walked up to the old square-towered church standing on a small hill, behind which lay a great slag heap. When they arrived, it was empty. The service was over rather to Tom's embarrassment, though not to the boys'. As they turned to walk away down through the old churchyard, they came face to face with the vicar, Tony Clemens, who held out his hands to them in welcome and asked who they were, and how far

they had come. Looking back now I can see so clearly that
from that moment the direction of our lives began to change
almost imperceptibly.

The following Sunday we all went across to church in
Newburn. Tony, I found, was impressive by any standard.
He was a man of dynamic character and unusual in many
ways. Physically arresting to look at, he had an infectious
vitality and humour, and almost at once the children loved
him. His presence had a power that could be felt and,
seemingly without effort on his part, he drew people to him.
He was an enlightened and brilliant evangelical who, after
serving in the Navy during the war, had studied for the
ministry. Fearless and forthright, but warm-hearted, he had
a hatred of cant and hypocrisy, and no use whatever for
false religiosity. He had a passion for souls. He quickly drew
us into his congregation, and we joined the church on the
hill.

It was inspiring to go to a church that was so obviously
pulsing with a new life. Often full, always expectant, its
atmosphere carried one along on a wave of enthusiasm.
"This is what I have been looking for so long," I sometimes
said to myself. It was as if the true church, meaning the
people, were bound together in a warm and loving and
listening fellowship, learning and sharing all that Tony gave
out to it.

Certainly he made demands on his people and on himself.
"I like the two-timers," he often said from the pulpit,
meaning those who were prepared to make the journey to
church – and often it *was* a journey – twice on Sunday. As
for himself, he had knocked on every door in his large,
straggling parish within three months of his arrival. If
anyone was absent on a Sunday for any reason, the phone
would ring on Monday morning, or he would make a point
of visiting their home.

Always supporting him in his ministry was a Church
Army chaplain, a real Tynesider who knew and understood
his people well, and whose great evangelistic zeal, coupled
with a sweetness of character, humour and humility,

endeared him to everyone. His task was to care for the little mission church at Blucher, up the hill from Newburn, an industrial sprawl of houses where any sign of wealth was notably absent.

Newburn in the last century had had its big houses and must have been a pleasant country village beside the River Tyne, but the Industrial Revolution had swallowed it up, transforming and obliterating its original character. Now it was mainly a confused conglomeration of small and shabby windy streets sloping up from the river, although outcrops of grass here and there, and an isolated field or two surrounded by houses, or the distant view up the river towards Wylam, reminded one briefly of what it had once been.

I was glad to live by the Tyne at Ryton, glad to cross the bridge each Sunday to the poorer area of Newburn where there was so much to learn and think about. Our children, who came to church with us every Sunday morning, were lively, restless, and full of energy. They might well have chafed at this regular Sunday routine, but in fact they too responded quickly to Tony's humour and vitality, and enjoyed his frequent teasing of them. Sometimes he let the boys use his air-gun in his large garden at the vicarage, a garden which lay almost in the shadow of the huge Stella Power Station. I think they knew instinctively that Tony really cared for his people, and they admired his strong, uncompromising and unusual character. Their obvious willingness to come to church as a family was a happy situation, because no undue pressures had to be exerted.

We soon grew fond of the people of Newburn as well as Ryton. They had a toughness born of adversity, for many of them had known poverty and suffering in the long years of the Depression in the North-East. They had a sturdy outlook on life compounded of earthy Geordie humour, forthrightness, loyalty and a capacity for hard work. They were never afraid to dirty their hands and tackle unpopular or difficult jobs. Once they accepted you they were friends for all seasons, and would not let you down. As for the women in the women's fellowship, which was run by Tony's stimulating and attractive wife Emma, they were delightful. They were homely, warm-hearted, and marvellous cooks. Any festive or special occasion saw vast quantities of home-baked sausage-rolls, scones, pasties, cakes and sandwiches. Their cheerful hot faces behind large tea-urns were full of welcome for friend and stranger.

During those first years, Tony shared many of his hopes and fears with Tom. He would walk the long three miles from Newburn, across the bridge, over the river, up the hill, through Ryton where the houses straggled for half a mile along the main road, and then he would turn down our road and appear, often unexpectedly, on the doorstep. He used to come in and sit in our large kitchen which looked out over the sunny garden, and where the family had the habit of congregating, and we would ply him with cups of tea and home-made cakes, while he teased the children or told us funny stories of the extraordinary things which seemed to happen to him. Then he and Tom would begin serious discussions, and the words of a poet would come to his mouth as he described his thoughts of what could be done in his parish which, by any standards, was a tough area. But Tony had visions of all that might be, and somehow had the ability to let others share them.

It was at Newburn that Tom and I were finally confirmed in the Church of England. Here we had found a spiritual home. Once more I had seen a reflection of the Holy Spirit in a place which was underprivileged and had seen bleak and terrible times. It was confirmation again that God was so often to be found in the dark places. I was proud and glad to know the people of Newburn, and to be part of their fellowship.

Life at Newburn church had many facets, and indeed was not without drama. It was a weird experience to discover that the vicarage, certainly at that time, was haunted. Tony's wife, Emma, had told me some strange stories about it, and it was a gloomy old stone house at the best of times. I think they must both have needed much courage and resolution to live there. One night I was sitting with her in the room next to the back door, which led to an enclosed backyard. It was a dark winter night, and I was waiting for David who was at a youth club meeting in another building. Suddenly I heard loud laughter – "rather nasty laughter", as Emma later commented – heard the back door fly open rather violently, and then heard voices of a crowd of people who seemed to be coming in. I thought it was David with members of the youth club and went to open the door of the room we were in, to save Emma getting up. I was totally astonished and dumbfounded to find no one was there. The back door was closed and the jumble of voices died on the air around me. I opened the back door. Everything was utterly still in the cold, keen, frosty air. I came in again and sat down, feeling silly. Emma looked at me in silence. A few moments later I heard the back door fly open again, and heard the crowd come in, and once again I went out to meet them. The same thing happened. When I reached the back door, the sounds died on the air. No one was there. I came in and sat down again. "Now you will believe what I've told you," said Emma quietly. A little later the back door flew open again. This time Emma spoke. "Don't move," she said. "You really don't know what you might see." It was then that I felt a strange trickle of fear, for as she spoke there came the sound, intensely clear, of high-heeled shoes tapping hard, as someone walked fast and purposefully through the long hall. Presently the sound faded. Everything was silent.

I cannot explain this. I only know it happened. But I believe certain sensitive people, similar to radio transmitters and receivers, pick up the echo of sounds and events of the past. It is an uncomfortable thing to happen but need not be fearsome, for in such situations I have found that appearances or hearings fade when Christ's name is mentioned aloud.

Rather strange and unnerving, too, was the experience of Chris, who gave us all a shock when he was about nine years old. We were sitting in the car just outside the vicarage, waiting for Tom. A friend and her son, a schoolfriend of Chris, were staying with us and we had been to church. Suddenly Chris looked very uneasy. He shifted about, got a little red in the face and said suddenly and anxiously, "Who are all those people quarrelling?" We could not understand this, as there was no sound of people to us. Chris persisted, looking odd. "I don't like the sound of all those people. Are they fighting?" Suddenly I realised he was most uneasy and had heard something utterly hidden from us. My first thought was to reassure him, and I said, hardly knowing what to say, "Oh, perhaps some of the youth club or choir have gone into the vicarage and are in the yard. I'll go and look." I got out of the car, hearing no sounds at all, looked into the backyard, saw no one was there, and knocked at the back door. There was no reply. The vicarage was empty, and obviously Tony and Emma were still over in church. I got back in the car; Chris was now looking most upset. "They're still quarrelling," he said. We all became silent. This was no joke, we realised. Luckily at this point Tom arrived from the church and we drove off. Chris asked him then about the "nasty people" quarrelling in the vicarage backyard. Tom instantly realised something was unusual and managed to calm him, as he could always calm the children with his quiet yet reassuring manner.

Again I have no explanation to offer, except that the vicarage is probably on the actual site of the Battle of Newburn which took place in 1640, when the Scots under General Leslie crossed the Tyne, seized Newcastle from the south, and occupied it for a year. The Puritan merchants of London and the South-East welcomed this invasion, which was one prelude to the Civil War. Had our son heard echoes of a past conflict? Extra-sensory perception is disconcerting, and often unwelcome. My mother had it, and experienced strange and violent impressions of the past in Glen Coe when we were staying there, and what she saw, we later discovered, had actually happened in the very place where she saw it occur, during the terrible massacre of the

Macdonalds by the Campbells. So perhaps it is a hereditary although unwelcome gift.

I do know that a service of exorcism was ultimately held at the vicarage. Since then I have not heard of anything untoward happening there.

After a time, Tom was made vicar's warden in Newburn church. He was always glad to help in any Christian work, and he gave himself to this as gladly as to any other of his commitments. Soon, urged by Tony, he started to study to become a lay reader at Newburn. At the time this seemed rather a special and significant step. After a great deal of work in his little spare time – for he was working exceedingly hard in the legal practice – he was finally commissioned in Newcastle Cathedral with a number of other men. He was chosen to read the lesson at the special service there, which meant, apparently, that he had gained the top marks of his group in the readers' examinations. The family turned out to a man to attend this service, but none of us, I think, had any idea then that his life really was beginning to take a new direction. Later he became a diocesan lay reader, and then travelled far and wide around the Northumberland countryside, enjoying nothing better than to take services in some remote country village.

As was inevitable, after some years at Newburn Tony left to go to a large and notable church in a more prosperous urban area. Before he went he had said on several occasions to Tom, "One day I think you should consider ordination. The church needs you so much." Shortly before he left he said the same thing about Tom to me. At first I laughed it off. He was sitting in our drawing-room at Ryton, and outside the window the garden was at the height of its summer beauty. The roses were a mass of colour, the rock plants were thriving and the cedar tree we had planted was growing steadily taller. To me that tree was the sign that this was to be our home during Tom's working life. I had always wanted to have a cedar tree in our garden, and the one at Barnard Castle, which we had planted when we lived there, withered and died slowly. Soon after that we had to leave and return to Newcastle. But this tree at Ryton was healthy and strong. I was sure we were meant to stay. So I laughed off Tony's uncomfortable words as wholly impractical. "Tom could not leave the family practice," I said, "and anyway I'd be a hopeless vicar's wife. You know I'm not really a churchy person at all." It was shadow-boxing, and I knew it. Tony looked at me very searchingly and smiled, but I felt a stab of something like fear, which I immediately tried to forget. The present was all that mattered, and it looked good.

Tony is dead now, but very recently he came suddenly and vividly alive again to me, when I heard our son David describe him in one of a series of broadcasts he gave on a B.B.C. local radio station, in a "Thought for the Day" series. Strong and assured, David's voice had something of the same vitality that I remembered so well in Tony, who had inspired him. This is part of what he said: "He had a huge shock of black curly gypsy hair, and walked majestically with a silver-knobbed ebony cane. He was vicar of Newburn, a tatty industrial Tyneside village, just near where I grew up, and under his ministry I was called to the priesthood. He was a giant not only physically but spiritually. He had the ability to make you know God loved you, and more, to make you aware God believed in you, and there was something only you could do. In fact Tony made you feel like a giant too; you walked taller for meeting him."

Yes, the lives of both Tom and David were to be irrevocably changed, and the effect on all of us was to be great. All this was to happen slowly and almost imperceptibly during our years at Ryton, and for me during that time Tyneside and its people were part of the very heart of our lives, and I wanted to live nowhere else.

5

The Happy Valley. An Interlude

Where Kielder Water is now beginning to stretch its ten-mile span along the bed of the North Tyne river, there used to be a beautiful valley, remote and peaceful. Now much of it has vanished, and houses and farms have disappeared under the encroaching waters of this vast, man-made reservoir as if they had never been. Here, in this valley, in the tiny hamlet of Yarrow was our holiday cottage, and here we planned one day perhaps to retire. It happened in this manner.

A few years after we went to live at Ryton, Tom took the road one day up the North Tyne to his branch office at Bellingham, a little market town some fifteen miles north-west of Hexham. He was in that area each week, and often on a spare Saturday took Chris fishing for brown trout near Tarset, a hamlet further up the river. He had taught Chris the art so well that he often brought home a better catch than his father. Both were such keen fishermen that when the fishing rights of that part of the river were sold, and they had nowhere to fish, the disappointment was great. On that particular day he heard of a small hill sheep farm for sale above Falstone, a little village further up the valley. A mile and a half of fishing went with it. He went up and visited it, and his imagination was captured.

That evening he casually announced that he had seen a small hill farm that was for sale at a very reasonable price. "Why did you go and see it?" I asked innocently, thinking it was something to do with a client's business. "There's one and half miles of fishing along the North Tyne that goes with it," he said in a sort of off-hand way. "You're never thinking of buying a farm, are you?" I asked incredulously. "Well, land is always the best investment," he said, "and Chris seems quite likely to farm one day, and land may well be quite impossible to get then. This is going at a most reasonable price."

Tom had always been both careful and generous with money, always putting aside anything he could for the children's future. Moorside, not being in one of the so-called fashionable areas, had been very reasonable to buy, and we had always lived simply, an inheritance, perhaps, of our puritan upbringing. So now I was astonished at what I was hearing. "You'd better come and see it," he said.

The next Saturday the whole family set off in the car. We drove miles past Hexham up the Tyne valley, and eventually branched off into the valley of its tributary, the North Tyne, which stretches up into the borders of Scotland. We passed Bellingham, and headed towards Falstone, driving along the road that twisted and turned beside the river all the way. At last, heading out into wilder country with forests on our left and outcrops of rock beside the road on our right, we came to the crest of a hill where there was a sharp turn into a little side road on the right. We turned here, descended a very steep hill, and saw a great panoramic view before us.

In a burst of sunlight through tattered, racing clouds we saw the river far away below, where it stretched in two sweeping curves past grassy, tree-covered slopes and open moorland pasture. The distant hillsides were covered with new forests, gashed by the broad "rides" which sloped up to the horizon. Down to our right lay a tiny cluster of grey stone cottages nestling into the hillside, with open fields behind them, bordered by dry stone walls. In the middle of them, standing a little back from the edge of a precipitous grassy drop to the rushing river below, stood a small, sturdy stone farmhouse, with a few stone barns around it. The farm, Tom told me, comprised 175 acres of moorland and rough pasture stretching westward, and twenty acres of good meadow pasture around it.

Within a month the farm was ours. Tom took over a flock of 130 ewes with it, mainly Scottish blackface, which are tough and hardy, and smaller and more wiry than lowland sheep, and better able to stand the severe northern winters. The price for all this, quite incredible as it now seems, would not today buy even a small house.

The little stone farmhouse would for a time, we thought, become our holiday cottage, where the family could breathe the fresh sweet air far away from the city's polluted atmosphere, and could learn about the practice and ways of hill farming on marginal land. This, Tom thought, would be invaluable to the children in later years, particularly to Chris. He appointed a young local man as his shepherd, to care for the sheep and do all the day-to-day work of the farm. The whole venture seemed extraordinary to me. It seemed such a daring thing for Tom to do. But I was to find years later how his forethought for the family would more than once prove invaluable. Meanwhile the place was so enchanting that I felt almost guilty at our good fortune and wanted our friends to be able to share it.

There was a lot to do before we could spend holidays and odd weekends at the farm. Tom said I must gather some very basic furniture of the very simplest nature so that we could camp in the little farmhouse and make it fit to live in, and this must be done quickly as he had to get up there at once and see that the sheep were doing satisfactorily. He had also to buy sixteen store cattle, as this was the number for which he could get a government grant, and he went to various stock markets with David and Chris trying to assess good beasts. It would be desirable to run these with the sheep, we learned, as this would provide the right balance of stock on the pasture.

Every spare minute for the next two weeks my job was to hunt through back-street junk shops and view cheap furniture at auction sales. My pride in purchasing two good oak bedsteads, one for a pound and one for thirty-five shillings, was enormous. I next bought some strong, light canvas camp beds, and a friend kindly gave us an excellent unwanted dining table and chairs. Another friend had a spare armchair which she gave us. Soon there was just enough for a very simple existence, and Tom said I must arrange with the local carrier to take it all up in his van.

It was at this point that things became complicated. In order that the cattle should calve in the late spring of the following year, it was necessary to have a bull to run with them on the moorland pasture. Tom took advice from various farming friends, and heard of quite a good black Aberdeen Angus bull which would be hardy and whose progeny should make good strong beef or store cattle. The bull must be taken up to the farm immediately, he said. He told me that I must contact the same carrier again, and arrange for the bull to be transported from the south-east of Northumberland to the farm which was in the north-west of the county.

I phoned the carrier, who had a rich Northumbrian lilt in his voice. "Why, that's nae problem," he said as I described the necessity of getting the bull to the farm as quickly as possible, "We'll just take him up with the furniture." I nearly dropped the phone. "*With* the furniture?" I said shakily. "Oh, ay, nae problem," he repeated. "I'll be up there by midday next Saturday." I was amazed and full of curiosity and reported this extraordinary information to Tom.

We waited impatiently for the weekend, and invited some

close friends, Bill and Doris, and their two boys and little girl Hilary, who had taken a great interest in the project, to join us up there for the day. The carrier was due to arrive about midday, and we clustered outside the little stone farmhouse, straining our eyes to look away towards the steep little road that led down to the hamlet. Presently the retired farmer, who had lived in a cottage close by for a number of years, appeared. Then his daughters and everyone else who lived in Yarrow began to stroll rather nonchalantly towards the farm. I was quite surprised and realised they, too, had all come to wait for our van. They certainly would not be impressed by our junk-shop furniture, I thought.

At last we glimpsed the top of a high cattle-truck van, as it appeared rocking and swaying between the dry stone walls as the vehicle very slowly descended the steep hill. "It's here, it's here," the family shouted, and everyone watched intently as it turned the corner and slowly came along towards the little crowd of people, and stopped just outside the farm. I was full of curiosity. *Surely* the bull could not be inside that van as well as our furniture?

The cheerful carrier jumped down and signalled to my husband and the locals to gather round with sticks. "Uncle Jack," as we all came to call him, the old farmer of the land, took up a sturdy position by the back door of the van, and Tom and Bill our friend, also stood at the ready. "Where's he to go then?" asked the carrier. "Through that gate onto the moorland pasture where the cows are," said Tom. "Right then, be ready to head him off," said the carrier. He released the tailboard of the van, pulled it down and, to my astonishment, a huge Aberdeen Angus bull was seen standing in a small compartment inside, not with, but clearly in front of our furniture which I realised must be behind a partition. It was a dramatic moment. The boys went forward with Tom. The little girls and I, and Bill's wife Doris, instinctively drew back. Would he be ferocious, or an amenable, quiet bull? In the event he gazed with dark brown eyes scornfully at everyone and climbed very slowly and ponderously down the ramp, and with the four men around him allowed himself to be guided to the gate that led out onto the moor, where the cows awaited him. I drew a breath of relief, having had visions of a bad-tempered bull running amok in the hamlet. Once he had seen the cows he was no longer interested in us, and indeed he lived a peaceful life with them for some years. A bull that runs with the cows is far less likely to give trouble than those that are deprived of female companionship, although if he is loose on open pasture it is safer to keep a good distance from him.

We returned to the van. The inner partition was removed, and our rather meagre bits of furniture were revealed. Courteously, everyone in the hamlet went forward to help carry them into the little farmhouse, murmuring words of welcome in their Northumbrian tongue. It was a happy day. Doris and I brewed endless cups of tea for everyone. The boys and the two little girls raced all over the farm. They ran down to the river, which sparkled in the sunlight as it tumbled over its stony bed, and ran in and out of the barns, and out onto the high pastures behind the house. All the while the curlews dipped and cried as they flew swiftly overhead, and the oyster-catchers swooped and played, their wings a flash of black and white in the sun, and a great happiness surged up inside me. Here in this beautiful place, only twenty miles from the Scottish border, I felt I had never been so aware of the beauty of God's creation. I would be able to be closer to it here in a certain way I thought, than perhaps ever before. I had felt the divine presence in times of sadness or difficulty, almost as if a loving hand was held out to support and strengthen. Now a feeling of pure joy came at the sheer splendour and colour of the scene, the distant blue of the border hills merging with the mingled greens of forest and moor, and the golden corn fields across the river and down in the valley towards the tiny village of Falstone. I felt a deep gratitude. Later that evening I went to thank Uncle Jack for his help. He looked at me with shrewd blue eyes in a tanned and weatherbeaten face, as if summing me up dispassionately. Suddenly I felt both ignorant of all the age-long ways of the border country, and totally inexperienced in everything to which his life had belonged. Slowly he took his pipe out of his mouth, shook it, and then turned and looked at me, and I have not forgotten his words, nor the cadences of his Northumbrian voice. "What are we here for, Mistress," he said, "if it is not to help each other?"

As the years passed and the children grew up, the farm became a loved place where we could go in holidays, or dash up for a night or two whenever we were free. Tom and George, the young local shepherd he had appointed to look after the farm and the sheep and cattle, consulted together on the best policies, and about each activity that must be done during the year's cycle. Eventually George needed a house, and with a little sadness Tom agreed he must live in the farmhouse with his pleasant young wife. For a time we went up and stayed in a caravan on the farm when we were free, and then after some years an elderly cousin wanted to have a retirement home near us, and a delightful small cedar-wood house was built in a field beside the farm, which sadly she never saw completed. It became, however, the loved place to which we imagined we would one day retire. Here the family helped with the hay-making, the boys learned how to dip sheep, and our interest in hill farming steadily grew, and has never left us.

From March onwards each year Chris loved nothing better than his fishing expeditions on our beautiful stretch of water on the North Tyne. Like his father, he loved wild and lonely places, and had a quiet patience that enabled him to become a keen and expert fisherman from a young age. I often used to wander down to the riverside at Yarrow and watch him from a distance.

Cathy greatly loved the farm days too. Accompanied by the dogs, she and her friend Hilary wandered the length and breadth of the farmlands and beyond. One favourite spot was a tiny sandy beach beside a very deep pool in the river, known locally as Ugly Dub, why I never found out, for it was a beautiful place sheltered by overhanging trees, through whose leaves the sun softly dappled the water, making it flash and sparkle in the light. Here, too, Chris often caught a good trout, and he would carry it back to the cottage where I fried it in butter, with a bay leaf inside it for flavour, and no fish ever tasted better.

Sometimes Chris fished further up the river, on a long open stretch of water where the river curved by stony beaches beside the moorland pastures. On the other side of the river, where fields grew golden as the corn ripened in summer, there were also pastures where cattle grazed right down to the water. On one occasion our bull, a Hereford by this time, actually waded across the river, which flowed quite swiftly there, neglecting his own harem, to reach the cows on the other side, and had to be driven back, and that was no easy task.

There was always a variety of wildlife. Often we saw a heron perch on a big rock that jutted up out of the water. Oyster-catchers and curlews cried overhead, and our sheep and lambs on the moor called continuously to each other as they moved to fresh grazing places. Strangely enough, they kept in two separate and distinct flocks, always apart, from some long, hereditary instinct ever since two smaller flocks had been amalgamated years earlier. Everywhere we walked we saw many species of birds, kestrels, sandpipers, siskins, goosanders, and a family of waxwings who were regular visitors to our wild garden.

On some days the family and their friends trekked off with a frying-pan, bread and sausages for a picnic to the little island, which was only about a hundred yards long, and lay about three quarters of a mile upstream from the farm in our stretch of the river. They would wade across, light a fire on the flat stony beach at one end of the island and prepare their meal. The island was a secret fairy place, half of it being covered by grass and sheltered by a dense thicket of small trees, in which you could be quite invisible. Expeditions to the island were dependent on the weather, and the river had to be low and calm, for after a storm the North Tyne used to rush down in great foaming torrents, almost submerging the island, bursting its banks as it roared down the valley, flooding the low-lying pastures, tearing down the low branches of trees, sweeping fast and furiously towards its lower reaches with tremendous and dangerous force as the water rapidly rose higher. Sometimes the road from Falstone to Bellingham was completely blocked by flood water, and one could only leave the valley by a most circuitous higher route, north of the river through many field gates.

Farming is a tricky business. Tom and David and Chris would visit auction marts at regular intervals and would purchase and also sell cattle when necessary. George would take sheep and lambs down to Bellingham and Hexham marts to sell. But after a few years it was clear that the venture was not paying its way. We had all learned an enormous amount about hill sheep farming, and had enjoyed every minute of our lives there. To our joy Bill and Doris had bought a cottage in the hamlet of Yarrow too, and Doris and I talked of the fun it would be when and if we ever lived there. At last Tom decided it was more viable to let the actual farm to a tenant farmer, and to retain our cottage and the fishing. This he did, and John and Shirley came to the farm, and were and are still a great asset to the whole neighbourhood, and eventually they bought the farm.

We still came up with friends whenever we could, and Bill and Doris's family and ours grew up together during the holidays. They had a pretty stone cottage down the steep little road which led past our house to the riverside, and they called it Yarrow Lea. Our small cedar-wood house was named High Pasture, for it stood on a ridge at the highest point of a huge field which sloped down eastwards towards the river and the tiny village of Falstone. A few hundred feet westwards from our house, over the dry stone wall of our wild garden, stood the sturdy stone farmhouse. In front of our house, outside the wooden garden gate, was the road and immediately beside it, separated only by a wire sheep fence, was a most precipitous grassy bank which dropped steeply down some two hundred feet to the rushing river below. On this bank Tom planted a variety of trees, which over the years grew slowly but steadily into a fine plantation, securing the bank itself more firmly and creating a haven for many birds and other wild creatures. The bright green young larches were my favourite trees, but the colours of all of them blended into a lovely pattern of pale and dark greens, varied by copper and red in the autumn.

On the clear fresh mornings of early summer I would get up and make a cup of tea, and stand outside to drink it while I looked over the young treetops on the bank, along the sparkling line of the river below that curved into the distance, and I would listen to the sound of the water rushing swiftly over its rocky bed making a wild music of its own. In the heat of the day I often walked upstream over the rough springy grass. One could almost always be alone there, surrounded by an immense quietness, broken only by the restless cry of a curlew flying overhead or the lambs crying for their mothers as the sheep moved to new pastures. Here one could sort out one's thoughts in the peace and stillness.

Every part of the land had a sweet familiarity. I knew every dip and hollow, every outcrop of rock, and as the sun set I used to watch the distant border hills turn from soft blue to gold. This was the hour when the forests beside the winding road up the valley to the village of Kielder nine miles away, stirred with secret life. Shy roe or fallow deer appeared suddenly, silently, sniffing the air, alert, heads poised, listening for the slightest sound that heralded danger. Then they would vanish as swiftly as they had come into the dark depths of the tall conifers, which stretched mile after mile across the land, forming the biggest man-made forest in Europe. One evening I saw a deer come out into a large clearing beside the road, and silhouetted against a brilliant red and gold sky it leaped and bounded to and fro with joy and secret ecstasy in every movement.

The North Tyne river became part of my life. It meant something very special. I felt then that whatever we had to do in life – and I had begun to sense that Tom had never forgotten Tony's words to him – the place to which we must ultimately return would be this valley. Even when working in the city or at Ryton, it pulled at the memory like a magnet, and one would be transported there in imagination, walking beside the river again and listening to the music of the water as it flowed over its rocky bed.

There was something symbolic about the very life of the river. Brought up by my parents on the words of the Bible from the earliest age I can remember, I had the matchless advantage of thinking naturally, even when very small, in words of great poetic beauty. I know now how rich that heritage was, for it formed a habit of thought that has never left me. So now when I wandered along the rough grass beside the river banks, I could hear instinctively the words of the Twenty-third Psalm: "He maketh me to lie down in green pastures: he leadeth me beside the still waters." When the river flowed down smooth and calm with scarcely a ripple on the water, it spoke to me of peace in heart and mind, and I remembered the words of the prophet Isaiah about Jerusalem: "For thus saith the Lord, behold I will extend peace to her like a river, and the glory of the Gentiles like a flowing stream." So thought patterns were often inextricably woven with Biblical words, and I could visualise the life of a good and God-fearing man exactly in the words of the writer of the First Psalm: "He shall be like a tree planted by the rivers of water, that bringeth forth his fruit in his season."

In this remote and lovely place, both Tom and I had time to read and to think, to pause and stand apart from our busy lives, and to see them in perspective. Most important perhaps, we had time and opportunity to ask ourselves what we still wanted to do with our lives. It was here, I believe, that Tom gradually came to recognise what he was, in fact, being asked to do; what to give up; and to what he was being called. For during these years he travelled the length and breadth of the North Tyne valley, both as a solicitor and, more significantly, as a diocesan lay reader, when he journeyed many miles, taking services in every parish of the North Tyne area.

It was the river, I think, that became most important to

me. It was a kind of symbol of life. I could watch it change from peaceful water meandering past grassy banks to thundering torrents hurling flotsam and jetsam before it. Our lives had, on the whole, been peaceful for quite a long time, and we had been unusually privileged to have such a place to come to. Many people had to live in dreary, depressing surroundings. Perhaps one day we, too, would experience a storm blowing through our lives, uprooting us, and we would have to leave this lovely place. For Christ's words came inescapably to me: "For unto whomsoever much is given, of him shall much be required." I knew in my heart that if indeed we were called to some special commitment it would be a sort of death to turn back. Present happiness would wither and die in face of the pain of loss if one turned away from God and rejected any endeavour to which one was called. "What shall it profit a man if he gain the whole world, and lose his own soul?"

Yet even with such thoughts that uncomfortably arose from time to time, I could not then know that our happiness in this remote valley was to be just an interlude, for only slowly did it become clear that Tom was indeed being called to give up the whole of his life as we knew it. Yet we would always be the richer for everything we had learned and experienced, and in a strange way that knowledge would help to fit both of us for the new life that lay ahead. Chris too, benefited greatly from his experience on the farm and from all the knowledge he gained. Years later, after college and travelling abroad to Labrador, he did become a farmer, although not in Northumberland, and his love of the land has never left him.

None of us could ever have dreamed that one day the vast new Kielder Dam would actually rise up on the very land that had been part of our farm; nor that the waters of the North Tyne, gathered here to supply the needs of hundreds of thousands of people on industrial Teesside miles way to the south, would drown much of the moorland and pastures of our happy valley for ever.

6

The Hurricane

"Something interesting is always going on in your home," a neighbour at Ryton said to me one day, "and it's often so unexpected." Certainly our lives were full of variety, and we had the normal joys and anxieties of bringing up a family. But it was true that events often took a surprising turn, and on more than one occasion something really dramatic and unexpected happened.

Yet at first we were hardly aware of the quiet and almost secret drama that was slowly unfolding, and beginning to affect our lives. It was when the boys were in their teens that Tom was beginning to feel that his work as a solicitor did not always allow him to help his clients at the very point where they were most in need. Again and again he found that their legal problems covered anxieties and troubles which were spiritual. Ethically he had to limit his work to that of a lawyer, but in his heart he often wanted to help them on a deeper level. The varied Christian work in which he was involved outside the office was obviously satisfying to him, but I believed he sometimes wished he could give his life wholly to some form of total Christian commitment, although I always felt that his influence as a known Christian professional man was of real value in the secular and business life of the city and the area around it. "I'm tired of helping people to make more money," he said to me one day. "So many people are basically sick in spirit, and my hands are tied."

It was, I think, like a shaft of sudden light to him when he received the letter that was being sent to all Newcastle diocesan lay readers, asking if, in view of the great need for more priests, any men cherished the desire to be ordained, or wished to consider ordination. If so, it was possible that an ordination school for mature laymen might be started in the diocese. After discussing this with me with obvious great interest but also with doubts, Tom eventually replied that he would like to take any course arranged, although he was uncertain if he could go ahead to ordination immediately it was completed. The response from the other lay readers was also very favourable. Many volunteered to take the course, which was eventually started and called the North-East Ordination School. It was scheduled to take four years to complete, as the work had to be done on top of the men's normal secular work.

As Tom began the work of the course, the challenge of it seized him, and grew steadily in his mind. Perhaps, he said once, to take such a step would be a culmination and fulfilment of his business life on Tyneside, where he had so many contacts. Many opportunities had indeed been given to him over the years as a solicitor. In addition to his ordinary work, he now held certain directorships, and he had been appointed by the Lord Chancellor to be Chairman of the Newcastle Pensions Tribunal. All this work he enjoyed, but I could see he was now driven by a further vision and by more distant horizons of the spirit. He had begun a journey and there was no turning back. Of one thing I was totally certain. Even if this eventually meant drastic changes in our life, I could not, nor did I wish, to oppose him in any way, because to do so would kill a vision that was clearly very precious to him. To ask him not to enter on this new work would have turned him into a frustrated and disappointed man. In any case I realised that he was determined to go ahead, and that having made up his mind, he would not be deterred.

It was now that I began to feel we had lost him in a way, for the time being. He was alone on a journey where we could not follow, but I could watch and wait with both eagerness and anxiety to see how things went. Now his life became almost impossibly full. He got up and studied for an hour or more before breakfast, set out to travel the eight miles to the city soon after eight o'clock, did a full day's work in the office as head of the firm, and returned about six for an evening meal with us. After this he vanished again to read and study and write. He had to go to evening lectures each week, and also to write long essays, do research, and think and evaluate all he had ever learned. But the new work fascinated him. He had always had something of the student in him.

David, Chris and Cathy took all this cheerfully. Dad was "a character". It was in keeping that he should do something unusual. They viewed his desire for total quiet and no disturbance humorously, although in a lively, often noisy house it was disconcerting. Finally, we thought up a plan. There was a little boxroom away from the rest of the house at the top of the stairs leading out of the kitchen, which was full of trunks, junk, old furniture and old toys. Secretly we cleared it out, cleaned it up, put down a little carpet that was surplus to our needs, furnished it with a desk and various bits of furniture from around the house, and put an electric fire in the tiny, old-fashioned hearth with its iron grate, dating back a hundred years, when the room must have belonged to one of the maids. One evening, when it was all ready, with fresh curtains and paint, and looking really quite attractive, we led him solemnly up the back stairs, and pointed to a humorous poem pinned on the closed door which exhorted all who approached to observe strict silence in the vicinity, and issued dire warnings to any who infringed this rule. Then we took him inside. Tom was delighted and very amused, and thereafter vanished into his new little study away from the family's noise and clatter each evening. For four years he studied here, entering new worlds which as yet were hidden from us.

As for the rest of us, our lives were broadening out and altering in the natural course of events as the children grew older. One change for all of us had concerned Newburn. Tony Clemens had left by this time, and we had for months been facing a conviction that grew in us. Deeply grateful as we were for the inspiration he had been to us and for new insights he had given us, Tom and I felt we really ought not to travel a distance to church with the family each Sunday, however attractive the ministry there. We had gained much at Newburn, and we were especially grateful that our children, particularly David, had been influenced by Tony's brilliant presentation of the Christian faith in today's world. Now we had come to feel it was not good always to seek a comfortable or inspiring church suited to our personal needs. It was far more important to belong to the church in the place where we lived and belonged. We are an independent family, each member having a strong streak of individuality and even obstinacy. Decisions are not influenced by outsiders. We now agreed that it was time to make some contribution of our own, if that was at all possible, in Ryton itself, and we believed we should fully join the parish church there.

It so happened that a new rector, John Rowlands, had recently come to Ryton. Wholly different in style and character from Tony, he had been an Army chaplain in the war. He had a matter-of-fact kindness, and a sturdy practical outlook on life. Tom went and talked to him, and from that moment, and indeed over the years, we were to be sustained by his support and understanding and friendship. He had come from being vicar of a large parish in industrial County Durham, and was fond of young people. Chris had a large group of friends in Ryton and soon they all joined the parish church choir, Chris included, which at the time quite amazed us, for he was a high-spirited boy often given to clowning, and to see him in choir robes solemnly processing into church on Sunday mornings was quite a revelation. Tom was often used as a lay reader in the district, and we enjoyed being among so many of the friends we had made in Ryton.

Our neighbour was quite right when she said our lives were full of variety, and it would be quite wrong to think that churchgoing dominated our existence. Far from it. On

Saturdays and in the school holidays there was often sailing on the broad waters of the Tyne at Ryton. When he was only about twelve, David had made a remarkable little coracle of wood and canvas, and this was launched with great solemnity one cold afternoon. Seeing him sitting alone in it as it rocked on the current – for the river flowed fast and strong there – I put up an anguished prayer for his safety as he was carried swiftly out on the grey cold waters. It would not be the first time I would do so. He seemed to crave danger, and was never happier than when he was engaged in some daring feat. We all watched him. Storm, our huge Newfoundland dog, a loved companion, stood looking out at him, and I felt that if he capsized Storm must be sent out to rescue him, for the dog often swam strongly in the river. However all was well. David returned triumphantly to the bank after trying out his little boat, and remarkably it survived a number of launchings.

Eventually Tom bought a second-hand Burnham Twelve, a small sturdy sailing dinghy, which he found at South Shields. Before he began his ordination course he spent hours sailing with the boys, particularly David, sometimes at Ryton, sometimes in the sea off the Northumbrian coast at Beadnell, just south of Bamburgh, and sometimes at Kippford on the Solway coast. Sailing entered into David's very blood. He became a keen and ardent yachtsman, and years later often went as a crew member in vacations on an ocean-going yacht. His room was full of his drawings and sketches of boats and yachts, and this interest has never left him.

Spring and summer days were long and happy, but winter in the north-east had its pleasures too. The family loved the coming of snow at Ryton, which often lay thick on the ground. They would get out the toboggan – and when they grew older their skis – and set off with friends to the sloping fields of a nearby farm or to the local golf-course. Storm loved the snow too, and on one occasion was harnessed to the toboggan on which Cathy clung precariously, while he romped through the snow. So life had colour and variety as the seasons passed, but on more than one occasion something happened which was totally unforeseen, and drew out of us unexpected emotion and response.

The most extraordinary event that occurred during the years that Tom was studying for his ordination course was dramatic and could easily have led to tragedy. It occurred one dark Sunday night when a violent and unprecedented freak hurricane hit the area.

At this time Chris was away in Scotland and missed the whole affair, to his regret. He had gone away to his public school when he was thirteen. There the rather spartan open-air life, the ideals of service to the community, the mountains and trout streams all around, helped to form a setting that suited him far better than a highly-academic large city grammar school, and drew out of him a positive response to everything he did whether in work or sport. He did well and was happy, and later said that if one had to go to school it was about the best place to be. His life in the Highlands developed in him a deep and lasting love of wild places and of natural beauty.

On the night of the extraordinary storm Tom was out taking Evensong at Ryton church. David and I were at home and Cathy was in bed with flu, in her room above the kitchen. The wind had been getting increasingly violent all the afternoon and early evening, and was quite unlike anything I had ever heard in my life. It howled and screamed around the houses, rattling and buffeting the windows and doors, whistling under doors, and the earth seemed to shiver and shake.

David, always eager for adventure, grew excited. "It's terrific," he said. "I think I'll put the sound on tape, I've never heard anything like it. I'll put the recorder just outside the window." He opened his bedroom window a bare two inches, and a tornado of air seemed to burst in and shake the room. But he got his recording as the wind screamed and moaned violently outside and the house creaked and groaned. I was glad when he eventually shut the window. I thought the glass might easily break with the force of the blast.

Then I went down to the kitchen to prepare a hot drink for

Cathy. Suddenly there was a very heavy crash outside the kitchen window on the garden side. Peering into the darkness I saw some shattered pieces of a very big Victorian chimney-pot lying on the rose-bed. Quickly I went up to tell Cathy not to worry for the crash was only a chimney-pot. As I was talking to her, another, louder crash was heard under her window. In the light that was streaming out from the kitchen below I saw another smashed chimney-pot on the path beneath. Cathy thought this exciting and was enjoying the thrill of the storm. So I went down the back stairs, which led from just outside the second door in her bedroom to the kitchen, to finish making her drink. Suddenly the whole house shuddered and with a crash a great deal of the plaster fell off the kitchen ceiling, all over me and the electric cooker, into the saucepan, and all over the floor. I shouted to Cathy, "Don't worry, it's only some plaster off the ceiling," thinking she might be dismayed by the noise. At this point the world suddenly seemed to come to an end. There was a tremendous echoing roar like thunder, just as if a huge bomb had exploded above my head, and totally aghast I heard what appeared to be the roof of the house falling in on top of Cathy above. Terrified, I flew up the back stairs and heard a tiny cry. I pushed at the door; it was jammed fast, presumably by falling masonry. I rushed down the stairs and out of the kitchen, shouting for David, "The roof's fallen on Cathy," and flew up the main stairs.

David acts in a flash in an emergency. Hearing me, he made one bound from his bedroom down the passage to Cathy's room, and when I reached the top of the stairs he was coming out of it holding in his arms a little limp body covered with soot and dirt. 'I think she's broken her legs, Mum," he said, tense and breathless. "I'll lie her on my bed." Gently he put Cathy down, and she cried a little and gasped and then was suddenly sick. I thought perhaps she had been desperately injured and was dying. We held her and wiped the soot and dirt from her eyes, nose and mouth, and cleaned her face, and black soot came off everywhere, all over David's bed. Then she began to talk a little, and we gently felt her all over. Having washed her, we saw her face was a deathly white colour, but she said, "I'm not really hurt, Mummy; the roof fell on me." At all costs we knew we had to reassure her, and keep her calm until we knew the extent of the damage. While I held her in my arms David went to see what had happened, and came back with the dramatic and rather awful news that her room was open to the night sky, and much of the roof and ceiling had caved in. I left Cathy momentarily and could only gasp at what I saw.

From the part of the ceiling that remained, an electric lightbulb, still alight, swung crazily in the wind. Above my head I could see stars in the sky where the huge stone chimney-stack had crashed through the ceiling bringing rafters, roof, masonry and plaster onto her, the floor and the bed. Massive stone blocks from the chimney-stack had crashed onto part of the bed, whose legs were now smashed and twisted beyond recognition. The pillow was covered with soot. The bedroom floor was submerged under masses of rubble. It was a terrible sight. I believed the weight of it would any minute bring down the floor too, into the kitchen beneath. Worst of all, I felt there was no hope that Cathy could have escaped without being very seriously hurt, and probably she was concussed anyway.

At this point, stunned and shaken, I remembered Tom. Where was he? Had he been injured? Frantically I called to him, for I thought he had come in from church just before the roof caved in. It was quite extraordinary, but suddenly as I called, he came out of the downstairs sitting-room half asleep. "What on earth's all the noise about?" he asked, rather annoyed. "Why is everyone shouting?" I was speechless, and only later learned he had come in so tired that he had fallen deeply asleep by the fire downstairs and had heard nothing of the collapse of the roof at the other end of the house. When he slowly took in what I tried to tell him he hardly believed me, until he came up and looked at Cathy. Then he was very shocked. When he saw the shattered bedroom he was incredulous. He carefully and gently felt her all over, and incredibly her limbs seemed uninjured.

Events seemed to move in a sort of blur after that. Cathy, lying very quiet, had no outward injury. Tom sat beside her. I phoned our opposite neighbour and friend. "Please could you bring us some hot very sweet tea in a flask," I said. "The roof's fallen in on Cathy, and the kitchen's unusable, and I *must* give her a hot drink for the shock." Winifred, my friend, could not understand what I was saying. Perhaps I was incoherent. But she and her husband Harold nobly struggled across in the storm, and when they came in and heard and saw what had happened they were appalled. Quickly Winifred rushed back and made hot tea.

Next, summoned by Tom, the fire brigade came. The men went upstairs to view the shattered room and to remove the masonry from the floor and hurl it out of the window as otherwise the floor would have soon given way under the weight. There were several of them and they were so helpful. "Well, it's fortunate no one was sleeping here," said one. "But they *were*," I said. "My little girl –" They could not believe it at all. "Well anyone would surely be killed," they said. Winifred and Harold said the same thing as they viewed the twisted bed. "For the first time in my life," said Harold, "I've seen a miracle. That child should have been killed. It's incredible."

We sat with Cathy, and ultimately Tom decided to sleep beside her. She seemed drowsy, and was reassured to have him. Nevertheless, I phoned our doctor, a very able and skilled physician, and a good friend. But he lived three miles away. He could not hear me properly on the phone. "The roof's fallen on Cathy," I said. "Well, I can't come, dear," he said. "A patient of mine here has just been blown right over a hedge and is injured. It's impossible to drive in this storm anyway. Give her an aspirin. What did you say had happened exactly?" The phone crackled and roared in the wind and I gave up.

Tom and David and I said our prayers by Cathy and asked for her healing from any injury. She fell quietly asleep.

The hurricane roared on until the early hours of the morning, then gradually died away. All night I felt ill with shock and anxiety about Cathy and could not sleep at all. At first light I went into her wrecked bedroom. "Dear Lord, thank you she's alive," I said as I looked at the wreckage. I went down and cleared masses of plaster and rubble off the electric cooker, put on the kettle and made tea. It was all unreal. Had it happened? Would Cathy remember this night with terror?

When I took the tea in, she was very pale but cheerful and lively. "Well, you'll have a tale to tell at school," I said, and she laughed at the thought. She seemed perfectly normal and her cheerful self. The doctor came later, and could hardly credit what had happened when he saw her room. He examined her very carefully, and found that quite miraculously she was totally unhurt. In fact she only had one minute scratch. Later in the day I felt it was possible to talk of what had happened. There was something I had to find out, because I realised a wonderful thing had happened. Surely something of a miracle had taken place.

"Did it hurt a lot when all the stones fell on the bed?" I asked as casually as I could. She looked up and smiled, and I shall never forget her answer, which came so simply and spontaneously. "No, Mummy," she said. "You see it felt like a lot of feathers falling on me."

"O Lord, thank you," I said in my heart, and could not speak as I saw her smile. I could only think of those beautiful words in Psalm Ninety-one that my father had often read to us on the bad nights in the war when enemy planes were overhead and we heard bombs dropping nearby:

> He shall cover thee with his feathers, and under his wings shalt thou trust: his truth shall be thy shield and buckler. Thou shalt not be afraid for the terror by night . . . for He shall give his angels charge over thee, to keep thee in all thy ways.

7

The Second Call

"Temporarily snowbound Gander."

The cable from Newfoundland arrived at the end of the first week in January, barely a year after the dramatic events of the hurricane, on a bitterly cold day when the snow lay in hard frozen ridges on the roads, and an east wind cut your face like a knife when you went outdoors. The three brief words marked the beginning of a real change in our family life.

Over a week before, David, fulfilling an urgent purpose which burned in him as strongly as Tom's desire for ordination, had flown out alone from Prestwick, heading for St. Anthony, Northern Newfoundland, where he was to work as a volunteer for the well-known Grenfell Hospital. This was the headquarters of the medical and social work of the Grenfell Association, known in former days as the Grenfell Mission. It had been founded by the great missionary doctor, Sir Wilfred Grenfell, known widely as

Grenfell of Labrador, whose remarkable pioneering medical work up and down the coasts of Newfoundland and Labrador earned him not only fame but the love and undying respect of the people of those wild and inhospitable territories which border the Arctic regions.

David had originally thought of studying law and following Tom in the family legal firm. But when he was sixteen Donald Marsh, Bishop of the Arctic, came to talk to the boys of the Royal Grammar School. He told them of the tremendous need for ordained men in that vast diocese. He described their travel by dog team sledges, on skis and snow-shoes, and in small planes that landed on skis on frozen ponds and lakes. Skidoos, or motorised sledges, had then barely arrived. The few roads were not made up and travel was very difficult. In winter the climate was arctic. Through his eyes David saw a wild, bitter, untamed land with a fierce beauty of its own, and from that moment, I think, home seemed dull, and the desire to go to the far North gripped him. I knew well that life in a lawyer's office might have seemed like a prison to a boy who so longed for adventure and travel and for every possible variety of experience. We urged him to take his university entrance examinations first and then consider what to do.

David proved his point two years later by winning an open exhibition in English to Cambridge, and had nine months before he was due to go up to his college. When the telegram arrived on Christmas Eve announcing his award, the family was thrilled, and David was pleased but not, I felt, particularly impressed. One thought dominated all others. "Now I *am* going to the Arctic!" he said. In the event it was Northern Newfoundland where he was accepted to work, after hectic phone calls to the London Headquarters of the International Grenfell Association. There were many last-minute arrangements, and he had to be kitted out in one week for an Arctic winter.

Tom drove him to Prestwick in bitter weather on the day when his plane was due to leave for Newfoundland just before midnight. The roads were ice-covered and it was sleeting. They stood together in the airport lounge. David had told us some months back that he felt he, too, had a call to be ordained ultimately. But first he said he must see the world and learn as much about life as he possibly could. So now two of our family were, in a sense, set apart in a special way. Strangely, I felt that I had been expecting this for a long time, and was not surprised. Tom said he felt numb and anxious when at last the flight number was called. David was eighteen but he was going entirely alone to a place where he knew no one. He was leaving us all to begin his own adventure in living. Father and son had both now, in different ways, had a Call, and from this time things would never be the same. I think both felt deeply for each other as they gripped hands and said goodbye, and David turned and left him. They had always been very close to each other.

Tom moved over to the big windows and gazed out into the darkness, and waited, straining his eyes until he saw the lights of the great jet as it began to turn and then move into the distance down the runway. At last it rose into the cold starry sky, and quickly disappeared from sight as it headed out across the Atlantic.

"I must have looked terrible," Tom told me later, "because the barman came over to me and said, 'Are you all right, sir? Can I get you something, a whisky perhaps?'" No doubt he was all too familiar with seeing sad partings, and the break-up of families.

David had promised to send a cable when he got to St. Anthony far to the north of Gander. We hoped we would hear from him in two or three days, but when no news came we began to get anxious. It was well over a week when the cable arrived at last, and we wondered how he could possibly manage in Gander as he had so little money. We wondered where he could stay. Had we known the truth we might have worried far more. The only hotel was far too expensive and after one night there, there was no news of the plane from the Grenfell Hospital at St. Anthony which could not get through because of the very severe weather and blizzard conditions. David began to search for cheap lodgings. Gander must have been a desolate place to land up in at the best of times. In midwinter it must have been a nightmare. Eventually he dossed down in poor basement lodgings, sharing a room with a drunken logger, and there he waited as the arctic weather continued. After a week, which must have seemed interminable, the small Grenfell Hospital plane at last got through, and he climbed into it and headed north with great relief. On the flight he watched the icy land of frozen lakes and snow-covered forests passing below. At last the plane circled and landed on skis on a lake in the township of St. Anthony, and in the cold, more bitter than anything he had ever imagined, David stumbled out onto the ice. "It's wonderful how warm it feels here when the temperature rises to freezing," he wrote much later.

For six months David lived in St. Anthony, part of the time teaching in the local high school, and also helping in the Grenfell Hospital as a volunteer. If letters came rather infrequently they were long and lively, and when they did arrive we caught glimpses of a totally different world through David's eyes.

> I went on a dog team trip to Goose Cove [one read]. We went sliding down the sunset, running by the sea, the snow crackling beneath the runners, and there was a cold smoky breeze. The Komatik is about eleven feet long, and fastened with lashings, not screws, so it gives to the bumpy ground. But Goose Cove trail is so bumpy that all the time the driver was hanging on with both feet off, trying to control the sledge on the downgrade. The horns on the front are for him to hang on to. When we reached a smooth bit he relaxed and fell overboard. When I got there it was late, so I was asked to stay the night. They are very hospitable in the small settlements. We had supper at six. Then another at twelve. And when I woke up I heard the morning for the first time here – birds, dogs waking, the sea breaking, and the wind breathing softly.

In those months David got to know many children in the orphanage and the patients in the hospital, many of them Eskimo or Indian. Tuberculosis was still a scourge in the far North. He wrote:

> Most of the patients in the T.B. sanatorium play the accordion. The young ones play jigs and reels, the old ones slow sad laments. About this time of year they start making nets for their boats, but many will never see the boats again. I play and sing with the guitar to the sanatorium children who have very little to do, and also to the children in the orphanage. And there is an old Eskimo in the T.B. ward with a guitar, who sings "What a friend we have in Jesus" in Eskimo, while I try the harmony. Good enough for T.V.

After six months David came home. He was asked to write in our church magazine about missionary work among the Esquimaux. When I read his article I seemed to hear again in imagination the voice of many of my forebears, and of my husband too, whose hearts were captivated by a vision of God which made all else in the world dwindle into meaningless insignificance:

> Donald Marsh, Bishop of the Arctic, speaking in Newcastle upon Tyne in October, 1960, said: "The work among the Esquimaux is your work because we are members of one church, and, whether in Jesmond or Northern Canada are God's people."
>
> A hundred years ago a little man fought his way North along the Arctic coast by canoe and sledge. For company he had only the cold Arctic sun and vicious northern blizzards – and his God.
>
> He stopped one night at an igloo, and, while the spluttering blubber lamp did its best to blacken the stretched intestine window in the roof, he told the family inside of "Our Father which art in Heaven".
>
> There was a little boy in the igloo, and although too

frightened to look at the preacher, he remembered his words. His father and mother just laughed – after all, everybody knew how strong the spirits were.

One day the little boy, now a young man, arrived at the first Eskimo mission house, built by Bishop Stringer on Nansen Island, and was converted. For seventeen years the converts were taught, then baptised as Christians with full knowledge of the Bible. Indeed, to an Eskimo, his Bible is his most important possession. As one said, "If I don't eat, I die, and if I don't eat spiritual food, I die inside."

The "little boy" stayed on at the mission station to help, and was eventually (1921) ordained the first Eskimo pastor.

When asked what was the greatest thing the English had done for Northern Canada, which is a country where industrial and scientific development has been immense, he replied, "Before the white man came to the Esquimaux they stole, and killed their children. Now they no longer do so."

Therefore we might think this Christmastide of the work for God in a country where snow is not a Christmas treat but a yearly environment.

The Bishop of the Arctic, while in Newcastle, appealed for "Helpers not Talkers". In Canada the parishes are often the size of England and an empty incumbency is more than a slight inconvenience.

Whether God calls us to traverse the snowy northern wastes by plane and dog team, or whether some task nearer home is ours, may we *not* say, "Lord, here I am, – send the other fellow," but "Lord, here I am – SEND ME".

We knew then that the boy had become a man, and from then on it was as if his eyes were always turned to far horizons. He went up to Cambridge later that year, and enjoyed his time there to the full, but it was for him, I think, an ivory tower where he could only pause for a while. The craving for adventure and new experiences never left him.

During his second year at Cambridge he was awarded a travel scholarship to go to Israel in the long vacation. The plan was to make an overland journey to Israel with five friends in a Land Rover, passing behind the Iron Curtain on the way, through Hungary and Rumania; and then to travel through Turkey. Through his letters home we caught the atmosphere of an unknown world once more and our world seemed bigger and more challenging because of this.

One night in Hungary, where the language barrier was total, the police moved them fiercely from their camping site for no reason they could understand, and took them to a peasant smallholding, indicating they must stay there. The old farmer was obviously terrified of them but, after the police went, signed to them that his field was no good because of the cows. He brought them into his tiny house and he and his family watched them intently and nervously. Now David and one of his friends, Martin, were both ordinands. Each night as they travelled towards the Holy Land they read a psalm together when they camped. The old peasant (so obviously scared), who had been watching them, saw them take out David's small red leather Bible, and read together from it, and suddenly a smile of pure joy lit up his face. He stepped forward as if to embrace them. It turned out he was a secret Lutheran Christian, and when he knew that they too were Christians his fear turned to great rejoicing. After that he kept coming into the room in his underwear, to nod and smile and wish them good night and God's blessing.

At last they arrived in Israel after many adventures, ready to stay and work for a time on a kibbutz. They travelled extensively in Israel during their time there, visiting the Dead Sea and journeying south to Petra. A short letter arrived for Tom's birthday. I have it before me now. It says:

We have climbed Mount Zion, we have walked the

holy places. – The holiness has gone: the shining of the
face of God cannot be caught inside buildings of stones.

Mount Zion is wherever, in feeling the sharpness of
the stones beneath your feet, you find the One who
walked them before.

And on its long rocky ridges may you look up and see
the Summit. Zion is where you are.

After David had taken his degree at Cambridge – in view
of his hope for ultimate ordination doing theology instead
of English in both parts of his tripos, which proved quite a
hard assignment – he said he would obviously be entirely
useless as a priest until he got more experience of real life,
perhaps at factory-floor level. So on the advice of the Dean
of his college he went for a year to the William Temple
College, then at Rugby, to take the first part of his General
Ordination examination. Then with the help of a Canadian
priest he met there, he went abroad again, this time to
western territory, first to take charge of a parish in Cariboo
diocese in partly Indian territory, during the absence of the
vicar on leave. There he was cared for by an Indian
housekeeper. The heat was intense. The parish stretched
eighty miles in length and there was no transport.

Of all his letters home during his first months in Canada,
one of the most vivid concerned the funeral of an Indian
child to which he went with Jim, the Canadian vicar friend
through whose initial contact and advice he had gone out to
work in Cariboo diocese. The letter seemed, in a way, to
describe something of the pathos and need in the world
which every ordained man must be prepared to face and
meet, trying to carry something of Christ's love to those who
so greatly need it. As we read it we were, once more,
transported far away. Our horizons broadened. I began to
feel that difficult as the future might be at times, we were
deeply privileged to be allowed to share in even a tiny part
of God's work. Perhaps it was a moment of enlightenment,
for the great upheaval in our own life was drawing

relentlessly nearer. This is what we read in the letter from Western Canada:

Jim and I drove twenty miles up the Frazer Canyon; at a distant ranch an old stocky perspiring Indian met us. He was carrying a home-made board, made of rough timber and rawhide – he was very proud of it – with the Eighteen Mile Community's week's provisions in cardboard boxes lashed to it, some eighty pounds' weight.

The normal river crossing place was in spate, so we had to climb down one thousand feet in a quarter of a mile, down the canyon banks, through tumbled rock-clinging pine woods – eighty degrees in the shade.

The far bank had completely changed in a week: melting snow had swollen the creeks, log bridges were all washed out, and a wreckage of stones and logs jutted right out into the swirling water.

The Indian showed us his boat, home-made of flat boards and rustic timber, the oars were planks nailed onto fir-trees. We set off rowing and in a minute we were flung downstream as far as the river was wide.

It is impossible to describe the far side: we had crossed two hundred yards and two hundred years. As we stepped ashore, a little wobbly, the forest was alive with smells and eyes. A loved forest, lived not just in, but with, Narnia.

A small Indian, and his son, slid out of the dappled shade – the father of the dead child. He moved his feet fast but gently as he led us through the forest, over the felled tree that would do until the bridge was put back – if ever. Jim, clerical-collared, over-balancing, we almost lost in the water.

We walked half a mile, and the father had a buggy waiting for us, the two raggledy horses sniffing and pawing in the shade of a bush.

Jim's now battered case of robes, and my haversack of Books of Common Prayer (Canada), were flung on and we rattled off. At the cemetery impassive relations waited. The new headboard, cut out of a solid tree-stump with a bucksaw and painted sky blue, was drying in the sun.

Empty port poorboys [water bottles] lay around.

The coffin did not go down; the father jumped in the hole and scrabbled. The insects buzzed slowly. The mother threw in packets of baby food – the child had a long journey to go. As the hole was filled, the spade turned up a broken feeding bottle and teat – provisions for another, longer dead, child.

Each member of the family threw in three handfuls of dust, and for the first time each one turned away and wept.

In the evening there would be a big party, a "Potlatch", plenty of cheap spirits, and maybe another family would forget their sick child, as this one had been forgotten until too late, or drive off the ferry into the river, or throw themselves before the C.P.R. express, as it howls through the canyon from White city to White city. And in the morning they would wander home, sadly drunk, or bitterly drunk, or just drunk.

For our journey back there were two horses waiting: we cantered slowly through the forest, just noticing car tops flash a mile away on the far bank. The people in the cars did not even know there was a world here.

We were paddled across the two hundred years, the dappled light closed, there was no more smell of sagebrush, and as we struggled up the one thousand feet, we waved and laughed at the swirling boat and at our last shared joke, that I could find my way by myself in the forest.

This land was their land: when the salmon and the cariboo came they accepted them, and when they went, they accepted it. Now they accept welfare with the same fatalism, and their spirit is broken. The totem poles are for the tourists.

Such letters were fascinating for the three of us at home. Cathy was still at school, and had come to a firm decision that eventually she wanted to take up nursing. Her adventures were still to come. She missed her brothers and with us waited eagerly for their letters, but there was one period when we heard nothing for a long time from David who was still in Western Canada. At last a Canadian colour magazine arrived through the post one morning at Ryton. A friend's son had sent it to his mother from Canada, and had marked an article in it for us to see. It described in pictorial and startlingly vivid terms the then fairly new but quickly-growing problem of the hippies who were arriving in throngs in certain cities, Vancouver and Toronto among them. The article featured a journalist and a young English ordinand, both in hippy garb, barefoot and walking through Vancouver, trying to get help in terms of food, accommodation, medicine and social welfare assistance from the civic authorities for the hundreds of young hippies whose life-style and problems were causing great concern. We had not heard from David for two months. He seemed to have vanished. Now as we looked at the pictures of the ordinand we got our first news of him. It was weeks later that several very long and disturbing letters told us a little of his story. While no one could presume to recount in depth so personal, so traumatic an experience as David had lived through, the bare bones of it were dramatic enough. The letters had to be read slowly; small extracts stood out, and the whole affair was to remain a sort of landmark in one's thinking. It would question assumptions, tear down preconceived notions, destroy some of our ideas of traditional respectability and stab us awake. It is still hard to read them, and no one but David can ever fully tell the story. I suspect much of it can never be told.

It began when he was working in an extremely happy and invigorating setting on the staff of the Anglican Lay Training Centre at Sorrento, British Columbia. He was invited to go during a vacation to a Labour Day Weekend Conference at Camp Artaban on Gambia Island, a camp built by a Christian organisation back in the Thirties. The topic was: "The Meeting of the Christian and Hippy Worlds."

"A hippy" David quoted, in those comparatively early days of Flower Power, "is in the eyes of 'straight', the new word for 'square', society, anyone who has long hair, wears beads, bare feet, outlandish and individualistic garb, who lives round 4th Avenue, (Vancouver), Haight-Ashbury (San Francisco), Yorkville (Toronto). The hippy will undoubtedly use drugs of some kind, probably L.S.D., and is without question a parasite on society and a social threat of the first magnitude. The rise of hippies is without doubt the rise of a sudden, more or less coherent, drop-out culture." "And", David wrote, "throughout Vancouver, city councils, rate-payers' associations, special committees amass thickening files on the subject. (The hippies stick to phials.) Everyone and his wife has definite opinions about hippies: the 'dirty hippies need whipping, deportation, bathing, discipline, to be buckled down to regular employment.' But", he went on, "*The real picture is much more complicated*." His letter continued:

Anyway, I and my friends from the Sorrento Teen Camp, where I'd been helping, set off for Vancouver. Emotional scenes of parting beneath the old pines and cedar. Behind, the lake, and on the skyline a glow and occasional burst of leaping flames: British Columbia's largest forest fire, 40,000 acres ravaged. The moon has turned to blood. Hitchhikers and beatniks have been commandeered into fighting it. In the morning ashes will fringe the lake.

The singing of "Auld Lang Syne", not bucolic lusty, but sad, aware; it has been one of the most moving Christian camps I have ever been to; and we grind off to Vancouver, an eerie weary night drive down the Frazer Canyon ... and there is the danger of falling rocks as the road scrambles into little shadowed canyon communities, the canyon sides so sheer they drip on the house shingle roofs, so high the top is almost unseeable from the car, (danger of dislocation of the neck).

At last Vancouver, civilised, respectable, pleasure-keeping, wealthy, wide green-lined streets. My friends rush me onto the Gambia Ferry.

After the ardent farewells, I discover that in their ardency I am on the wrong boat. I end up at a little port called Gambia Harbour – no boats go any further. No boats go back. The camp is on the opposite side of the island. There are no roads, nothing but bush.

Then suddenly my world becomes like a strange dream, full of sudden and beautiful things . . .

I start talking to an old bent man on the jetty: it turns out he was the chief engineer on the *Mauretania*, the best ship the Tyne ever built. He offers me a bed for the night. The rest of the little community arrives; I am introduced to someone's extended family . . . I am taken home . . . a beautiful blonde with a speed boat is produced to take me to the camp. Water hitch-hiking, I decide, has it over the other kind any time!

Camp Artaban cabins are like nothing but Chinese opium dens, ten hard wooden bunks crammed into a twelve-foot building without doors or windows, just holes.

In rather sad, typical church fashion, there are no hippies to join us in the dialogue, everyone is lost, not sure how to discuss . . . who are hippies, why, anyway? The place feels like people lost in a railway station just after an air-raid . . . really a weird atmosphere; perhaps we are all part of some huge rat-like experiment. In the main cabin food appears and disappears, hard to tell how. Are we being watched, analysed? Langorous brown photos of long dead clergy peer down from the walls – are they watching too? No one living arrives to organise, greet or explain . . . my friend Peter needs the lavatory . . . a woman helpfully remembers, "I was here as a girl twenty years ago, I think it's this way . . ." but it's not. It has been demolished.

Sunday. Some hippies did arrive, very courageously, I think, to be thrown to the Christian lions: the latter keep asking fanged lion questions, as much excommunicating as communicating.

There are four hippies: two without shoes, Lenny with long hair, Ernie with beads, bangles, a watch and a little bell around his neck, Jim with, as his only worldly possessions, a box of his poems and a pair of drumsticks, the Colonel with a bedding-roll, a cowboy hat and waxed whiskers . . .

I lose my temper with the discussion and blow up . . . things get better. We are really talking to each other now.

We discover the four are "diggers" (from "dig", to understand), a group among the hippies who attempt to feed, clothe, and shelter the others. All this is fascinating sociologically; a new society is inchoately developing social institutions, and is trying to be responsible for itself.

We begin to respect each other; hippies are looking for a new way of living together and loving each other, new realms of freedom, new authentic experiences. (Is this close to what a church should be?) The difference: the opting out of a competitive capitalist system, etc.

Monday. Things are happening. We begin to do strange little weird loving things for each other. We wake the oversleeping hippies with gentle flute and guitar music – they remember weeks afterwards gratefully. People bring me my toothbrush in the mornings, they put flowers in my hair, they bring me food. The sensation of dreaming becomes stronger, and the feeling of reality too . . .

The weekend is finished . . . an ancient steamer carried us back to the mainland. Someone produced bagpipes and played reels and laments; we danced and felt. A wistful end; the hippies suddenly sad and aware that the Christians could be as "hip". And the Christians went back to comfortable North Vancouver homes with carpets and stereos. The hippies to Fourth Avenue, where no one quite knows where the next night's sleep will come from, on what grim or happy floor, or where tomorrow's meals will be. And few bagpipes or flutes.

They asked me to join them.

David decided to move to Fourth Avenue:

A solemn decision. Fourth Avenue is a rather seedy street in the west end. Besides several thousand hippies there are several "hippy" shops: Rags to Riches, selling home-made sandals among its goods; the Fat Angel, for custom-designed hookahs; the Psychedelic Shop, for so-called psychedelic arts and knick-knacks; and the Village Bistro, where the owner finds hippies can make a straight night out memorable. (Rent a hippy, only $3 an hour, harmless and entertaining.)

Terrifying and harrowing adventures, await your copy now.

We read fascinated, apprehensive, knowing full well that wherever he could go to meet people in love and understanding, David would go. It seemed an eternity before the next letter arrived. We read:

Joining a hippy scene is a journey into humility: discovering the poor naked forked two-legged thing man is, stripped of his suitings, society's apathetic self-respect.

The scene: the low-rent appartments, Chinese grocery stores, undesirable commercial properties, and peeling ornate timber houses with wooden, WOODEN! fire escapes and mock-tile tar-paper roofs run down to the KITSILANO BEACH, a yacht club at one extreme, a maritime museum at the other; and in the middle an

imposing public urinal in the modern style. And for
children like me a 4-4-0 wood-burning LOCOMO-
TIVE, first on the Canadian-Pacific run, preserved in
the civic park. But the beach mostly, you undertand,
just sky space and sea space, grey sand, and drifted
cedar trees – horizontals and lonely clouds . . .

Here I went seeking Lennie, ("Meet me at the
FEED-IN on Kit's beach.") No one had seen him, of
the sleeping, gently talking, quietly coupling bodies on
the beach. Other events: passing the urinal, a rational
reassuring disembodied male voice from the window
on the women's side, "Could you get me out of here?
We seem to have been locked in." "They seem to have
been locked in," I told the attendant. His lips were
tight and white. "*I* locked the door. There they stay
until the police arrive." Which was soon (black sedan
with red light).

I turned back for the Rev. Geoff Archer's.

Wednesday. I looked for Lennie at the address he
gave, in battered Albemi Street. Yes, Lennie had been
there, but it wasn't his house . . .

I met a man who knew a man who knew someone
who knew Lennie. I followed the underground scent,
now feeling like a new member of the French
Resistance, or the early church – to West Third Avenue.
"This pad grooves peace", I read on the door.

In a tiny basement room were twelve diggers
discussing. Imagine the scene: the wild eyes; the
furniture: one rotten bed frame, an electric ring and a
wood box. The people: Spider (the way he walked)
with a tooth necklace, shoulder-length hair, zono hat,
huge boots and a little dog on a string; Dragon (every
time he took an acid trip – L.S.D. – he saw dragons);
Earl, with a big badge, "When I'm dead send me
home"; besides Lennie, Jim, the Colonel and Ernie.
For all the world like a committee business meeting
they are discussing "among the smells of perspiration,
garbage and marijuna – the sweat, refuse and dreams

of the poverty stricken": – the problems of Runaway Girls, No Food, No Money and No Place To Go. The only place to go is here: a forty by twenty foot earth and concrete sub-rented basement, free crash-pad for homeless hippies. "The runaway girls," they said, "we can help them; they trust us. Man, we can't hand them over to the police; maybe we can talk with them, help them, keep them in contact with their parents. The welfare, the police. It's a bad scene, man."

Spider gives his testimony: "Man, I had everything – wealthy home, chauffeur to take me to school, private tutor . . . never saw my parents . . . I couldn't take it. Now I've nothing and I'm doing all right."

Earl: "I've been on the road since I was fourteen."

Dragon: "We can do something. I feel needed here. I've been 'inside' too often. I can't do any more time: I'd kill myself first." (He probably would.)

VISION suddenly grows . . .

We, Society's rejects, can change our world with our love. Half the kids on Fourth don't know what it's about, we can show them.

ACTION.

Communications with Welfare, the city, tell them what we're trying to do.

All at once I am made a public relations hippy.

Outside the scream of a police siren.

And so Saturday night came, and David, wrapped in his greying Sorrento blanket, lay down on the hard cement floor among crowds of hippies, lost kids and runaways, and entered their life. he wrote a description of this:

Lennie pushing dope and acid: everybody high. Teenyboppers switch-backing nightmare and ecstasy: "Wow, I'm high", a fifteen-year-old went on interminably to anyone who would listen. "Everybody's stoned to the eyeballs – have you ever seen so many beautiful people?" another said.

Chuck pushed me to drop acid, but Lennie said, "He doesn't need it, man. Dave's high all the time – on God." Suddenly I am humbled by the hippy compliment.

On the Sunday morning the diggers rented the house where they had sub-rented the basement. David commented:

The house is now an explosive mixing-pot of *true hippies*: easy to talk to, pacifist, understanding, loving. *Weekend Hippies*: teenagers wearing beads and bangles, lost, unaware of the ideas behind it all. *The really lost kids*: deviants, delinquents, society's rejects, thrown out of home or school or job. Some with acute emotional problems, under-age runaways, pregnant girls. *Wolves and Greasers*: sort of rockers, with black leather jackets, swastikas, jackboots with chains, tattoos, "Born to Raise Hell", or "D.M.C." (Devil May Care).

On the Sunday night, he wrote that the police had raided the house, and there was panic among the hippies. The penalty for marijuana possession was about six months in prison. But no dope was found in the house. It had all been hidden in the garden.

On the Monday, he wrote, "Jim and I are seeing social workers, community officials, clergymen, trying to work out the best way to deal with our problems, and with runaways." "We were," he wrote later, "two barefoot scruffs hitch-hiking Vancouver and treated like the wise!! Come to think of it, I've done more counselling here in a day than some must do in a week."

He stayed with the hippies for some weeks, meeting many tragic runaways, and heroin addicts, including Caesar, of whom he wrote, "Every six hours or so, Caesar screamed and writhed as he tried to kick his heroin habit 'cold turkey' – a solid torn human flesh focus for the terror behind. God, may they not find him with a bullet through his head too."

A terrifying situation had now arisen with the hippies living in fear of a Mafia-type drug-pushing syndicate. More than one of the young drug addicts had been shot, possibly knowing too much. David sat by Caesar. He wrote:

> He was brought up by his aunt whom he feared and hated. The one thing he needs is a SUPPORTIVE COMMUNITY – and this he can only find in a God-forsaken underworld which survives a hand-to-mouth precarious existence . . . God-forsaken? Ah, Lord, I forgot: where in Heaven do we find you but in Hell? The incarnation . . . Christmas. And look, here's a real chick, Frenchie, become totally involved with Caesar's agony, by his side twenty-four hours a day . . . and she's becoming more gentle; something beautiful is happening. John, an ex-hospital orderly, and "The Mad Englishman" (a zany, neurotic, lovable, lost immigrant who couldn't find work) have become Caesar's medical staff.

After his weeks with the hippies, the time came for David to travel on, for his visa was expiring. He wrote:

> And now it is midnight. I must go to Kamloops. I feel guilty to be spending $7 when I could be hitch-hiking with my blanket and haversack. And so much I have left undone. And so many people left undone by chance or carelessness.
>
> And I buy a coke from a machine and in the middle of the garish bus station Jim and I drink from the same paper cup. And these things are a very holy mystery, and I am forgiven.
>
> And so I leave. The bus grinds through the Frazer Canyon in darkness, and at dawn we are in Cariboo country and the sun rises over the sage-brush. I had forgotten it was so beautiful.

When eventually David returned home after his year in

Canada, he went to Queen's College, Birmingham, to take the final part of his General Ordination examination and also to work there for the new Diploma in Pastoral Studies, which was to involve a good deal of social work in a large prison and in a hospital.

By now, Tom had nearly finished his own ordination course, and was directed by the diocesan authorities to go for some months to the theological college in Durham. He was coming closer to the traumatic moment of leaving his fine city practice, with its two country branch offices. Since the war he had built up the business with great energy and care, and had a real concern for his clients. He had worked hard and unremittingly. He would leave work that was dear to him. But, like David he, too, in a different way was looking to far horizons and a new vision, and he was prepared not to count the cost.

8

Irish Adventure

Ireland has a sweet magic. In these tragic times of the troubles it is well to recall the memory of it, for it coloured our lives more than once during the years when Tom was studying at his ordination course, and it was in Ireland that we spent our last holiday all together as a family.

We had let clergy friends use our cottage by the farm for a much-needed holiday, and, through an advertisement, rented for two weeks a house on the shores of Dunmanus Bay, just south of Bantry Bay on the south-west coast of Ireland. The final inducement which led to this decision was the words at the end of the advertisement: "Use of rowing boat with outboard motor".

We crossed by car ferry from Fishguard to Cork, a long night crossing over a rather choppy sea. As we drew into Cork harbour we heard the church bells chiming and echoing across the sky.

When you land in Ireland, you realise at once that you are, in a sense, in a foreign country. Life is timeless. It moves to the steady rhythm of a pulse or heartbeat. There is no unseemly haste, no urgency. Every passer-by on the road pauses to exchange a greeting or ask where you come from. We drove westwards through County Cork, along quiet winding roads and lanes, where the hedgerows were full of flowers and everywhere the whitewashed cottages and gardens were splashed with the vivid red of fuchsias. The sky was brilliant blue, with white cumulus clouds sailing high overhead. The incense-sharp smell of peat smoke hung over the villages, and every so often there were little wayside shrines with bunches of flowers under a large crucifix, or a figure of the Virgin Mary.

We reached the west coast at last, with its undulating hills and distant views of blue mountains, and entered the little village of Durrus. Here we made for the small general stores where we had to pick up the key of our house. The store, we found, was literally the heart of the place, selling everything one could possibly imagine or need, and full of stools and benches for customers, for in the evenings it turned into a kind of homely little pub during the hours the Irish happily called "drinking time". Here we received a great welcome as only the Irish can give it. Lovable, silver-tongued and innately curious, they made us feel they were overjoyed to see us, and fascinated by our every move. "You are blessed," they said as they handed over the key. "You have a beautiful family." Everything must be for our pleasure, it seemed. Tom asked two men in the lane just behind the pretty white house that was to be our home for two weeks whether the fishing was good locally. They pointed westwards. "Why, sorr, if you just go to that little bay past the first headland," they said, "you'll find the fish lying there, just waiting to take your hooks!"

The house stood alone among fields beside the water on the arm of the sea-lough. On the sea wall outside the front windows we could sit or stand and watch spectacular views across the water, and awe-inspiring sunsets. The weather remained improbably Mediterranean day after day with cloudless skies and great heat. Who had said Ireland was always wet?

Each morning I cycled to the shop on a hired bike to get the milk, and settled down on a stool, as was obviously expected, for at least half an hour's chat while the various other goods I wanted were slowly forthcoming. I learned much from these leisurely morning sessions. The grocer's wife was an attractive lively woman, eager to exchange views and ideas. In this Roman Catholic country I found the English in general were regarded as dissolute and highly immoral because of our permissive society and easy divorce laws. Conversations were always extremely friendly. I had to be ready to consider her points fairly and put my views forward if necessary. We were greatly favoured in their eyes as special people, it seemed, because amazingly to them, both Tom and David were hoping ultimately to be ordained. I found myself bound to admire the apparent total stability of family life in this village, whatever peccadilloes individuals might commit. Moreover the place was so peaceful. Violence, it appeared, was unknown. Even quite young girls, including the grocer's attractive dark curly-headed daughter aged twelve, could walk or cycle alone anywhere in safety we were told. The priest was still clearly a very powerful character in the life of the village. This gave me much to think about. "It is very sad about cities like London," the grocer's wife said. "There is so much wickedness. But of course they have not the faith." I could not disagree.

I settled down to enjoy a wonderfully relaxing holiday, as I thought. As usual I had not bargained for the family's inability to keep out of hair-raising adventures. This time the central character in a new saga was Tom.

The state of the small boat we found tied up to the sea wall just outside the house might well have alerted me to trouble. Its clumsy oars turned out to be no more than roughly-fashioned cut-off branches of trees, and their performance was extremely erratic. The outboard motor was unreliable, and water seemed to seep gently through the floorboards. But I did not think much about it, because on the roof-rack of the car we had brought the precious long Canadian canoe, made many years earlier by Tom's solicitor father, a great fisherman and canoeist even into his eighties, and now lovingly repaired by Tom and the boys and repainted silver. It was large and long, graceful in line and unusual in shape, and had a very strong double-ended paddle, made early in the century of hard, highly-polished wood. Each morning Tom, still immersed in theological studies, climbed into it, together with a pile of books and his recorder. Over the water there then would come the sound of his piping – psalm tunes and hymns mostly whose sound floated out from small hidden creaks where he drew in to read or meditate.

In contrast, David would often sit on the sea wall, playing folk music on his guitar with verve and gusto, and there was a swing and a beat about the music which sent the blood surging and feet tapping. Meanwhile Chris would often be fishing nearby, and Cathy could always amuse herself with her brothers, particuarly when by the water, and she often took the canoe for a short way herself, or sat in the little rowing boat trying to manipulate the oars. It was all very relaxing and pleasant.

One day my peace was shattered. David had become restless and eager to take the small boat right down the sea loch towards the open sea. "I'm sure it's not safe," I murmured fearfully. "Don't fuss, Mum. It's not at all bad, and we've got the outboard motor," he answered. I looked apprehensively at the sky. "The weather's changing," I said lugubriously, but I was soon shouted down. It was decided that Tom, in the canoe, would follow the rest of us in the boat. David took his seat aft, by the outboard motor. I clambered in gingerly as it rocked and swayed perilously and sat in the bow, and seized the baler which I felt sure would be needed. Chris and Cathy sat on the two centre seats, ready to use the clumsy oars if necessary. The engine, after some persuasion from David, spluttered into furious life and catapulted us forward and out into the loch. David turned the boat and headed her out into deep water towards the sea. Skimming the water behind us, the silver canoe shot forward out of a tiny creek where Tom had been waiting for us, piping and reading as usual.

I saw with sinking heart that storm clouds were beginning to mass and move towards us from the west. A sudden wind

buffeted us, but David steered the boat relentlessly forward.
Water began to slap against the sides and splash over the
gunwale as we moved quite fast down the loch. Ahead the
formerly silk-smooth water was suddenly covered with
ruffles of white foam. "This is great," said David, oblivious
of everything except his pleasure in handling the little craft.
I gazed straight ahead for a long time, apprehensively
measuring our distance to the shores on either side of the
lough which were rapidly receding and leaving us alone in
a broad waste of increasingly turbulent sea water. The sky
grew heavy and grey, and a few drops of rain fell. The wind
grew stronger.

Suddenly I became aware that complete silence seemed
to have fallen on the boys and Cathy. I turned and saw that
they appeared to have been struck suddenly rigid, turned
into stone, and utterly still were gazing fixedly at something
behind the boat. I turned in the direction where they seemed
to be looking so intently and was immediately horrified.
There in the water some way behind us was Tom, fully
clothed swimming towards the boat. As I looked, papers
and theological books swept past us on the water; then his
precious wooden recorder whirled by, too far away for us to
reach out for it. Clearly he had capsized in the increasingly
rough water, but where, oh where was the canoe? Suddenly
I saw it upside down, like the back of a shark, shooting past
us towards the sea.

The boys kept quiet and calm, making great efforts to
turn the boat towards Tom. Chris leaned out to try and grab
him when we got near enough. But the sharp turn of the
boat in the stormy water nearly capsized it. It rocked
perilously and we were all in danger of falling sideways into
the lough. At last it lurched and righted itself. Then a
terrible moment came. The outboard motor spluttered,
coughed and died. We started to float further away from
Tom, who, I felt, must find swimming impossible in all his
clothes, and he had no life jacket on, which he always wore
if on the sea.

Some frantic moments ensued. Chris and Cathy wrestled

desperately with the very inefficient little oars but the tide was now running so strongly that we hardly seemed to move at all. As usual Tom remained totally calm, shouting crisp, concise instructions to the boys as he swam, advising them how best to handle the boat. I was by now baling the water out of the bottom of the boat, for it suddenly appeared to be seeping in dangerously fast. David worked endlessly at the motor. After a time that seemed like eternity the engine flared into life again and we reached Tom. But he is a tall man and was now totally waterlogged, and the weight of water in his clothes almost pulled the little boat over as he held on to it, and tried, with the help of the boys, to haul himself over the side. David, Chris and Cathy held on to him like bulldogs, but we rocked most perilously, and again and again it seemed he could not make it.

Cathy and I now took the oars, and David left the engine entirely to lend all his weight to try and haul him in. At long last with a mighty heave and cascades of water he almost fell forwards into the bottom of the boat.

Now the nightmare journey back up the lough to our house began. We were far from the shore. The sky was stormy, we were buffeted by squalls of wind and rain, and again and again the engine stopped. Tom, obviously very chilled in his soaking clothes, and the boys worked desperately to move the boat with the tree-branch oars. It was a mighty struggle.

It seemed an eternity later, but was, I suppose, about two or three hours after the capsize of the canoe when at last we rowed into calmer waters near our white house at the head of the lough. The kind Irishwoman who, as part of the owner's arrangement, came twice a week to "do" for us, cleaning, and baking delicious soda bread, rushed out of the front door when she saw us approaching, almost wringing her hands. When she saw Tom, streaming with water, she flung them up in horror. "Holy Mother of God, I thought you were drowned. Thank God you're all safe," she said, rolling her eyes heavenwards.

As we went indoors the smell of the new bread and the

feel of firm ground beneath our feet were like a benediction to me. I said my own private prayer of thanks to the Lord to whose loving care I so often committed my adventurous family. I had a shameful feeling of acute secret pleasure that the canoe had been washed away, out to sea, for ever I hoped. I felt sick of all boats. But I might have known – the family always wins in the end.

Later that day, towards evening, Tom said, "We'll drive down to the coast now and look for the canoe." "It must be miles out to sea by now," I said hopefully. "Well, we'll have a look anyway," he said.

We drove some fifteen miles down the coast and there was no sign of it. I was just beginning to be privately jubilant, when I saw something on the distant beach of a small bay. It shone silver in the evening light. There was a triumphant shout from the boys. We reached the canoe lying on the rocks. It only had a tear in one side. "That will be quite easy to repair when we get home," said Tom cheerfully, as everyone helped to hoist it on the car roof. Clearly, like the family's spirit, there was something indestructible about it.

On our last evening in Durrus we all went down to the shop by request. It was now turned for the evening into a little pub. One or two shepherds, wrinkled and weather-beaten, had come down from the hills, and their collie dogs lay at their feet. A few men from the village were there, and the grocer and his wife were presiding over the gathering. David had been asked to bring his guitar, and Tom and Chris had drum sticks and wire drum brushes which they were going to attempt to use on biscuit tins, no real drums being available. At home David and Chris played the guitar, and with their friends had formed a group called the Border Raiders, and were often in demand. Now they had been asked by the grocer's wife to sing some Northumbrian folk-songs to everyone who was gathered there. It was a memorable evening. The music was fast and merry and sad by turn, as many of the old songs and ballads were sung, and everyone joined in when David taught them the words. At the very end there was much clapping, and then suddenly and unexpectedly David broke into the music of an old Irish lament, written during the time of the tragically disastrous potato famine in the last century. He sang alone with deep feeling and sincerity, and then everyone softly joined in the refrain. I saw in the evening light the glistening of tears on the men's rough cheeks. It was a moment when barriers were crossed, grievous memories were shared, and there was love and friendship between us.

It was quite dark when we left. The soft warm air, heavy with the scent of flowers, caressed us, and our way home was illuminated by the soft yet brilliant glow of a huge harvest moon rising slowly above the hilltops. The grocer's wife had flung her arms around us all, kissing everyone. "Oh, we cannot say goodbye," she said. "You must come back to us sometime."

"That's what it's all about," I found myself thinking as we left the shores of Ireland next day on the big car ferry. "It's relationships with people that will matter more than anything else when Tom is ordained. We must be willing to meet them wherever they are, to learn about their lives, to share joys and sorrows, and that's something that I can share in, too." Just then I felt elated. We were going to be entrusted with a very special task.

9

One Who Serves

The slim man in a grey suit stepped hesitantly out of the shadows behind one of the massive Norman pillars at the back of the nave in Durham Cathedral that morning of September 22nd, 1968, as the large congregation slowly moved down the aisles towards the open door through which the light streamed in, turning the dark stone to pale gold. The great Ordination service was over. A number of men had made their most solemn commitment, some as priests, some, including Tom, as deacons, "men ordained to serve". Friends and families were waiting to surround and greet the men, and to wish them well. The man in the neat grey suit seemed very much alone, but his intelligent eyes were searching eagerly among the crowds. I was standing near him, with the family close by, and wondered why he did not seem quite to fit into the setting, and why he had the look of a stranger from some far-off place. Then I saw Tom, his face alight with a kind of deep inner joy, coming towards us, and any doubts I might have had about this great step he had taken were finally silenced.

Tom suddenly saw the man, turned and went straight to

him, holding out his hands. The man came shyly up to him, and I heard him say, "I had to be with you on this special day. I wanted in a little way to share in your happiness." It was only later that I knew the real significance of that moment which has stayed so vividly in my memory. For this was a client whom Tom, as a solicitor, had over the years constantly tried to help, even when his life repeatedly went wrong and he had had to serve prison sentences. He had, in fact, only recently been released. Tom had visited him in prison, had counselled him and advised him. Eventually he had told him about his own faith in Christ that had held and sustained him over all the years and through all life's difficulties and challenges. He had told him of the only One who could wipe out failures, hold out forgiveness, and make new men and women of all who put their lives in His hands. Now Tom introduced him to us as a valued friend, and we all shook hands. The boys looked most unusually formal and smart in their best suits, and had red roses in their buttonholes, a characteristic touch of gentle flamboyance for their father's great day. Cathy too had put on her prettiest dress, and they all stood smiling by their father. I could not be too grateful for their warm-hearted support, often so humorous in expression, but always totally loyal.

Bishop Ian Ramsey of Durham, whom so many of us came to love and admire not only for his vast intellect, but perhaps especially for his outgoing warmth, simplicity of style and loving understanding of ordinary people, had ordained the men in a service full of beauty and colour and music, but so awesome in its commitment that I felt humbled to be able in a special way to share in it. The solemn words of question and answer still echoed in my mind.

> "Do you think that you are truly called, according to the will of our Lord Jesus Christ, and the due order of this Realm, to the ministry of the Church?"
> "I do."

"Will you apply your diligence to frame and fashion your lives and the lives of your families, according to the Doctrine of Christ; and to make both yourselves and them, as much as in you lieth, wholesome examples of the flock of Christ?"

"I will so do, the Lord being my helper."

Yes, the die was cast. There was no turning back now. As we stood there the final chords of the organ thundered and reverberated up into the remote roof arches and as the sound slowly faded it seemed like distant echoes, not from the past but from an unknown future, like a far-off voice calling us out into the unknown,

The months before the Ordination had not, in fact, been easy. Tom finished and passed his ordination course examinations which had taken the form of many essays. It had been arranged that before he served his first title he should go to theological college for a short, very concentrated course, and to this he looked forward very much. It was a terrible time of testing when, as the weeks before the Ordination passed, no title where he could serve was forthcoming. He was now repeatedly told that it was difficult to find the right place for such a senior man, that the whole position in the Church of England had changed dramatically and many parishes were being amalgamated, and the numbers of clergy were being cut down. Originally Newcastle diocesan authorities had asked that the men on the course should promise to give five years to the diocese, and this was exactly what Tom wanted. No one had a more intimate knowledge of the North-East, or a greater interest in its people. Tom had responded to the call for men to be ordained at a time of great need in the church, as the authorities had declared, not only because of his desire to work for God full-time, but also because he felt that to work as an ordained man on Tyneside and in Northumberland would be a fitting culmination to his professional working life there.

The time came for Tom to hand over the family practice

to his partners, after detailed and careful arrangements for all his clients had been made. The farewell dinner for him at a Newcastle hotel, the speeches, the parting from his large and loyal staff, was a moving occasion. Tom, his father, grandfather and great-grandfather had all been solicitors on Tyneside, so this meant a very big break for him. He had, I think, cherished a hope that one of the boys would follow him in the family firm, but it became increasingly clear that neither felt this was his choice of a career, and it was our desire that they should choose their own way of life, and do what they felt right for themselves.

As we waited for news of an opening where Tom might serve, we heard of other men on the course also in the same predicament. They had given up good and often fine careers to answer a challenge, and now began to wonder if they were wanted at all. I knew of several wives who were under great strain, and others who were having a dire struggle to support their families as their husbands went off to theological college. A number had gone back to work, leaving grandparents to care for small children. As the days passed I saw that Tom had begun to be very anxious.

Shortly before Tom finally went to Cranmer Hall, part of St. John's College, Durham, for the final concentrated weeks before Ordination, I met by chance our rector, John Rowlands. I was becoming very distressed by Tom's disappointment at having, as yet, no prospect of anywhere to go. "Why, oh why," I had asked myself angrily, "did the church authorities ever suggest this ordination course and encourage such senior men to take it, if they did not make very sure that they could keep what was in effect a promise to offer titles to them, and let them work in their own area for five years or more?" I found myself pouring out these feelings to John in a way I had never done before. I shall always be grateful for the staunch, positive and practical support he gave at that time. His words remain in my mind, for I know how clearly he must have seen my anxiety. "I'm blazing at what they're doing to Tom," he said. "I myself would love to have him here as my colleague, I need one right enough, but the parish can't afford a curate. Still, we'll see. I intend to go and see the bishop over the water as soon as he'll see me, and sort this out." Ryton was, of course, just inside the boundaries of County Durham, lying beside the south bank of the Tyne. Newcastle diocese lay "over the water", on the north side of the Tyne, until further westwards it covered land on both sides of the river. Tom's legal practice was in Newcastle diocese as was his old family home, and he had hoped to work in that area. However, we had now come to love the neighbouring Ryton area, and felt completely at home there. We next heard that John, getting no assurance at all of work for Tom in the northern diocese, had gone straight to see the Bishop of Durham.

From that moment the position changed. Ian Ramsey, with characteristic warmth and kindness, and, it must be said, in charge of a bigger and historically far more important diocese, said that he would love to have Tom working in County Durham at Ryton, and interviewed Tom, giving him his blessing. It was arranged that the diocese would pay Tom a very small stipend, far less than a curate's usual income, but Tom was content, knowing that Ryton parish could not afford to pay him. For three years, probably, we would have to live on our savings, and Tom's care and forethought in business meant that we should just manage. We both had the settled conviction that this arrangement was wholly right. In fact a greatly reduced income has been a challenge, rather than a disadvantage. Now Tom knew he was to become John's curate, whom John sensitively called "my colleague". Ryton was growing rapidly, and as rural dean, John had had no curate and was very busy and needed help. This was a wonderful answer to our problems and prayers. Now, for a time, we would be able to stay in our own home while Cathy finished her schooling. Tom would be ministering to people of whom we had grown very fond, who had, in their down-to-earth way, supported him in all he was doing.

This arrangement meant that Tom was able to go happily to his residential course at Cranmer Hall Theological

College. It was an exciting and inspiring time for him. He needed a time of quiet for study and prayer apart from everyday concerns. Perhaps unexpectedly, I found this time a hard test for me. Wives were totally discouraged from visiting their husbands while they were at college, except for one open afternoon when we all had tea and played croquet on the college lawn, and one afternoon which did not prove at all memorable when talks were given to prospective clergy wives, followed by some uninspired discussions. I felt that for mature couples, with growing families, sudden complete separation could have brought real tension. I asked if we could briefly visit him just for an hour or so on Saturdays, chiefly for Cathy's sake. This was not, it seemed, acceptable. Yet there were a few women as well as all the men in the college, and there was naturally a good deal of happy social life; but the wives left behind, some carrying heavy burdens of responsibility for their families, were barred from any of this. I believe this is changed now, and that husbands and wives can have residential accommodation together in some colleges and in any case keep in close touch. I am sure that this is right.

I was fortunate in having many interests and much absorbing work which helped to carry me through this time. I had been doing some part-time teaching in the grammar school in Newcastle where I had had my very first job. I had also been privileged to work as a city magistrate for a number of years, with particular concern for the juvenile court, and was lucky in having many fine colleagues and friends. Perhaps the most interesting job was in connection with a boys' approved school (now a community home), in whose work I was particularly involved. My job often took me to the school within the school, and I frequently visited the classrooms, and got to know a number of the boys. Often their background and stories were terrible, and some were desperately in need of help. Others were hard-line young delinquents and it was impossible to get through to them. Now when our home during these weeks seemed empty and silent, and when Cathy was at school all day, I was particularly grateful for such outside stimulus and work, which helped to fill the time.

Being often at home alone meant that I sometimes thought over the implications for our lives of Tom's ordination which was now almost on us. I have always found introspection distasteful, being too busy with living each day to the full to want to indulge in it. But certain conclusions seemed obvious. My job, as I saw it, was to be the helper. I could back Tom up and try to create a home that was a welcoming happy place where people would like to come. Of course, that was what I had always tried to make it, so on the whole I was quite relaxed about that aspect.

I really was willing, too, to manage on a very greatly reduced income. Over the years we had been careful, and Tom had worked very hard. We had, you could say, been fortunate. I had seen so many other people have a real struggle to make ends meet. Now it was our turn. In some ways I welcomed the challenge, although at first I found it hard to get rid of my small car which I had used for travelling to the various places where I worked. "We must just share one car," Tom had said. "A curate can't possibly afford two cars." This I quite understood. The war years had, of course, taught us the great value, indeed the strange delight, of travelling light, and of not counting on material possessions for satisfaction and happiness. I believed that, in face of Third World poverty, it was vital that Christians should show themselves willing to adopt a simpler life style.

There would possibly be problems of a different sort if I ever became a vicar's wife, I thought. I knew well from observations, and from friends, that parishioners very often have many false expectations of the rôle, which are virtually impossible to fulfil. They can try to force you into a mould of their own making. This can make life most difficult and lonely. Obviously the important thing, therefore, was just to be yourself, totally sincere and natural, and not to feel that you were in any way special. Some people put vicars' wives on a sort of pedestal, hoping that their own needs would

somehow be fulfilled through them. Sooner or later the
pedestal will crack. So, I felt, I must always keep my feet
firmly on the ground and reject that approach.

These thoughts seemed just common sense to me, and on
the whole I felt optimistic about the days ahead.

Then something happened, and I had to face the whole
situation again and to see it with different eyes. I had
sometimes wondered if Tom thought I had not really
counted the cost of all that his ordination might mean. The
retreat to which he and the other men had gone immediately
before the service in Durham Cathedral was taken by
Canon Sidney Evans of King's College, London.

The day before he was ordained, Tom phoned me, to my
great surprise, to say Canon Evans had most kindly
consented to see me too. Tom was clearly anxious for me to
go. I was at once apprehensive. I could only suppose it must
be to talk over any spiritual problems, and this is something
I have never found at all easy. Indeed, I have never wanted
to do it. I felt I could find all necessary help and guidance
from the Bible which so often spoke to me, both when I
studied it for teaching, and when I read it alone. Sometimes
the words stood out, and seemed to speak so directly. I did
deeply believe that I could seek God's help in all situations.
But I really did not want to probe into the matter too
profoundly with a stranger. Would the interview be a sort of
confessional, I wondered.

In the event Canon Evans was kindness itself. He gently
drew me out, and I found it was not difficult to talk to him.
I told him that I always preferred working in secular
situations. To me all life is one, and I felt there should be no
false demarcation between sacred and secular. So perhaps,
I said, I was not particularly suited to be the wife of an
ordained man, for this and other reasons. But I could say I
was wholly behind Tom, would support him in every way
and greatly desired his happiness in this great venture. I
remember I said, as I had years earlier to Tony Clemens,
"I'm not a very 'churchy' person, but I am a committed

Christian by belief. I know I often fail, but at least I really like people and am happy to have open house."

Now I have said everything necessary, I thought; surely it was enough. It had been rather a happy interview. I stood up to go.

Canon Evans looked at me long and thoughtfully. Then he said after a pause, "How do you see *your* ministry? Do *you* really share your husband's commitment to Christ?" I was silent, and could almost feel myself backing away from the questions. I did not want to be so disturbed, so shaken from safe moorings. But the time had come when at last in that quiet room I had to look into my own heart. It was my faith that was in question, and as I thought over all that had happened, the realisation slowly began to dawn that perhaps the unexpected call had come to me too, and that an answer was required. I do not remember what I said, but years later I tried to write down my personal credo, an answer to the questions that on that day rang so insistently in the silence. I remember it was painful to face oneself, stripped of one's thin regard, of the mirror image, and to feel vulnerable, nothing, a ghost. But the realisation of emptiness can be the very moment of discovery.

This is what I wrote:

I have always had a deep and terrible fear of loss. Mostly it is hidden. Perhaps, I do not know, it stems from very early days when my mother left me to go away to a hospital for a long time. She nearly died.

But no loss on earth can compare with that of total separation from Christ, the source of our being and our life. Without Him the loneliness of life would be total, an annihilation. Paul puts it a little differently. "If Christ be not raised, then is our faith vain." The great Resurrection truth is my hope.

I know I cannot live without Him. If outwardly I appear self-sufficient, capable, determined, busy, inwardly I am afraid; I feel inadequate; I have a need to cling; I am a child crying in the darkness.

It is then that the darkness thins and fades. I see a figure of indescribable beauty. I cannot look up. My hand is taken, and I am held. He is here and His presence is healing. He gives me strength for weakness, and joy for sorrows. This is the Lord who has guided me in life. Whenever I turn to Him, He is waiting. He died to bring the beautiful gift of forgiveness and peace, and in His death is my birth.

To all who call to Him in repentance and need He brings new life, salvation. This I know and believe, for I have held out my empty hands and have received His love. How little I deserve it. So many things have been left undone. But I am forgiven and my life is renewed. In Him I am not alone.

And now a miracle: I look at people not with my eyes, but His. I am given a love for them that is not my own, and I must pass it on. They need it so much. He looks at me from the faces of children, from the sad eyes of the lonely, the poor and the hungry. Am I ready to carry His compassion to them? "Inasmuch as ye did it to one of the least of these, ye did it unto Me."

There is another miracle: I see His beauty anew in the living world, bright as on the first day of Creation. I see Him in the sun and moon and stars. His voice is in the wind and waters. He spreads out his colours across the earth. He speaks to me in the silence of the night.

Lord, thank you that you allow me to recognise you in all life. Give me, all unworthy, your love, your patient love, so that I may pass it on to all I meet; to the young and eager who need to find you; to the lonely and lost who search for you with longing; to those who watch and wait in anxiety and sorrow.

I am here, Lord, use me.

On the day of the Ordination such difficulties lay behind us. "Probably," said Tom, "it was very necessary that our faith should really be tested before I went ahead." I looked around at all the friends who had come to be with us, the large busload of warm-hearted Ryton people, the Newcastle colleagues and friends, Tom's sister and her husband, and many close friends who just wanted to support him, and I was full of gratitude. The man in the grey suit had surprised and touched us by his parting remark as he slipped away into the shadows of the cloisters: "When you were out a few days ago, I went and planted a lot of spring bulbs in your front garden. Think of me when they come up in the spring."

There was one other person I cannot forget from that day. One of our Ryton churchwardens – a forthright man, who had worked at the pits as a check-weighman, and who stood no nonsense from anybody, but who had a fierce loyalty to those people in whom he believed – came up to me. He had an expression I had never seen on his face before, because he was never a man to show emotion. Now he was obviously moved and found words difficult. At last he said, "Mrs. Arnott, when I saw your husband come down the aisle in the great procession after the ordination, there was such a look on his face that I began to understand a little of what all this day means to him. I shall never forget it until my dying day." We gripped each other's hands, for I knew just what he meant. It was as if something great and glorious had touched Tom. There was a radiance about him that I shall not forget all the days of my life.

10

Facing Up To It

After the day of the Ordination, I began to see our home with different eyes. It had subtly changed, for now it was the curate's house, and I felt it likely that people would come there with problems and troubles to see Tom, and so it proved. I began to perceive that ordained men have made at least one sacrifice that some people find hard: they are no longer private people, but have – or should have – made themselves available at all hours of the day to any who are in need. Tom welcomed this. He wanted to be used in any way possible, and now found that, quite apart from helping with services, he was able to make new and deeper relationships with some of the people in the parish, helping them in different situations.

I did not at first imagine that my own life would be greatly changed during the years of his curacy at Ryton. It was stimulating to be still involved in all the interesting work, quite outside the church, that had come to me. I have always been wholly convinced that Christians should engage themselves in the work and life of their own communities when possible, and should not retreat into some cosy spiritual ghetto. However, I made a resolution to be particularly regular at the Sunday services in Ryton church, and to support Tom and John Rowlands in any way possible.

I was blithely optimistic again about the future, and indeed Tom and I still imagined that after the years at Ryton as a curate, some small living would be found for him in Newcastle diocese, as the Bishop of Newcastle had told him, even though no title had been found for him as a curate. This had been confirmed by the Bishop of Durham who had told him that Durham diocese would train him so that he could eventually return to the northern diocese. I often pictured vividly in my mind some little stone vicarage in the country in Northumberland, with a garden and a rural community, and thought how pleasant life there might be, although I knew it would be difficult to leave Moorside. Meanwhile it was good to be still at home.

I did not dream then that two things were finally needed to change my life entirely before I could in any full sense understand and share Tom's work.

The first was the writing of a book, *The Brethren*, which was the story of my childhood and growing-up in a Plymouth Brethren home. Tom had urged me to put down memories of my early days in writing while he was working for ordination. I suppose I had sometimes inwardly felt that I had been forced into a puritan religious mould by my father, of whom I was greatly fond. But it had been difficult to find freedom to seek God in my own way. When I knew Tom was to be ordained, I sometimes felt that in becoming a vicar's wife I would be forced into yet another religious mould, and in the process I felt it would again be difficult, if not impossible, to be myself. Tom knew this, and in any case I could joke about it, but he took it more seriously.

"You've got a chip on your shoulder about your childhood," he said. "Write it down. Get it out of your system," and then with a grin he added, "it will be much cheaper for me than a psychiatrist's couch!"

"I could never write all that down," I said. "It would be embarrassing."

"I think it would be very interesting," he said. "You've always said you would like to write, but you don't get on with it."

I was stung into action and started to put on paper what I imagined would be a few gently humorous memories of a puritan home; what it felt like to be "a meeting child"; pictures of some of the unusual characters I had known.

It was then that something remarkable occurred. It was suddenly as if another hand took the pen. If I was going to tell this story, I found I could not just do it lightly. I must tell only the truth. Once more in memory I stepped across the threshold of my home in the beautiful Georgian city of Bath, saw the rooms inside, and the people there, heard the voices that had so long been silent, and listened, and watched, and re-lived those years as vividly and in as great detail as if they were happening while I wrote. In many ways I knew it was a poignant story and I had not intended to write any of that side of it. Now it all came pouring out, and I sat at the kitchen table surrounded by paper, while often the meals got late, and I was totally lost to my surroundings. The family were benign and amused, and obviously felt that I was harmlessly engaged on a new venture, and should be encouraged.

When it was finished Tom was quite enthusiastic about it, to my surprise. I sent it to a publisher, and it was returned, but there was an encouraging letter with it. Then Tom mentioned it to a lay reader friend, a director of Mowbrays' publishing house at Oxford. He asked to see the manuscript, which I was convinced would be of no interest to him. Eventually I sent it off. It then appeared to get lost, as I heard no more for three months. At last I had a remarkable letter of encouragement, but was advised that I should write a little more to complete and to round off the story because, in the view of Canon William Purcell of Worcester, literary adviser to Mowbrays, who wrote to me, it was not finished, and certain questions were left unanswered.

"I just can't write any more," I said to Tom.

"Well, that's very silly," he answered. "I think he's right."

A week or two later Tom was at church one Sunday morning. I was at home with Cathy, who was in bed with a feverish cold. I sat at the kitchen table once more, where I always write, and described the events of the war years when Tom was in the Navy, and when my parents lost their home and all their possessions in the very heavy air-raid on Bath. I wrote of my parents' great courage, and eventually of their death. I found I was crying as I wrote, tears that kept falling on the paper, but I was writing so fast that I could not stop to wipe them away. I was lost to all around me.

When Tom came back from church the book was finished. He read it and urged me to send it off at once. I shall never forget the letter that came one week later, which told me it had been accepted, and that Mowbrays planned to publish it.

Tom had been right. It had been "cheaper than a psychiatrist's couch". In re-living the past I seemed to have experienced a sort of remarkable healing of memories. Now I could be truly grateful for my parents' total Christian commitment, from which I knew my own inadequate faith stemmed, and I realised that their commitment must be mine also. Past and present need be severed no longer, for they had become part of one pattern, which was still in process of being created.

I hardly know how to write of the second happening in my life, which was deeply personal and was to change it for ever, for no words can adequately describe it. How does one express that which is outside earthly experience? In humility and awe I can only say that it is integral to this story and that the spiritual healing, which began when I started writing and another hand seemed to direct my pen, was completed in a way that was dramatic and totally unforeseen. Theologians might say that I had to be broken before I could really live. Tom says simply and with certainty that the Holy Spirit touched my life. I know he is right.

After *The Brethren* was published, I was stunned by the flow of letters that started to arrive. Most I found very moving, for to my amazement they kept thanking me for sharing experiences and inspiration, doubts and difficulties, in which the writers all felt they had a part. It seemed I had unwittingly been a sort of catalyst of the hidden emotions of great numbers of people, many of whom now wanted to share their stories with me. One of the most remarkable and unexpected letters came from Mrs. Jean Coggan, wife of the then Archbishop of York. She told me how much my book meant to her, "for," she wrote, "I found I was reading the story of my own life." She asked that we might meet sometime, and this happened a few months later at a large gathering at St. John's College, Durham. As a result, I am privileged to say, I grew to know her as a real friend. We had shared an almost identical upbringing in the setting of the Plymouth Brethren and at sister high schools, until at different times we were both at London University. Our great pleasure over the years since that first meeting lay in the understanding and laughter we shared as we recalled very funny moments from childhood. Yet we had both been held and inspired by an unbreakable staunchness of faith in our mothers, both vicar's daughters, and in our fathers, both medical men distinguished in their own spheres. Over the years since then, her friendship and encouragement have been a sustaining factor in both Tom's life and mine, as has that of her husband, particularly when he was Archbishop of York.

A few months after we met, she invited me to the Clergy Wives' Conference at Scargill, one of a number she organised. Scargill is a lay community based on Scargill House at Kettlewell in North Yorkshire, and set in wild and beautiful countryside just below the crags and fells of Wharfedale. I felt apprehensive at being among so many clergy wives, but yet eager to meet people, and learn more about the strange new life on which we had embarked.

In the event the conference was one of the best experiences of my life. The speakers, including the writer and theologian-housewife Rosemary Haughton, and Jean Coggan herself, were excellent. Discussions were constructive, helpful, and at times very amusing. Free time was spent in many creative projects. For some reason I find difficult to understand, I signed on for a sort of music and movement group in which emotional responses to situations were played out in music and dance. At times this was hilarious. At other times I realised that it gave a sense of release and freedom. It appeared we were supposed to be ridding ourselves of stress. It was fascinating to watch the wives, many of whom must have worked courageously in difficult situations, really let themselves go. Age did not seem to matter. The most elegant performer in dance, I remember, must have been in her fifties.

I was happily enjoying the conference, interested in so much that was being said. I found incredibly funny some of the odder problems that wives encountered in their husbands' parishes. One wife, whose husband, like mine, had been ordained in middle life and who now found being a vicar's wife intolerably difficult, said to me, "My dear, I had a terrible time. Almost the first day we arrived at the new vicarage a woman came to the door and said, 'Now you've come, you'll wash the purificators, won't you?' Well, I simply hadn't a clue what a purificator was, and when it came to the albs and amice and goodness knows what else, I was simply finished!"

"Well, what on earth is a purificator?" I said, adding, "I know absolutely nothing about church linen. I just can't imagine being responsible for it!" We laughed and I began to realise my great lack of knowledge in church matters, and felt much cheered by this companion in ignorance. And there it would all have ended. I would have left the conference happily, exactly the same as when I arrived. But at lunch on nearly the last day something happened.

I found myself sitting next to a clergy wife who looked desperately pale and ill. I did not know her at all. When she

read my name on the little badge we all wore, she started
violently and looked as if she were going to faint. "Are you
the Anne Arnott who wrote *The Brethren*?" she asked. I
admitted with a little embarrassment that yes, I was.
"Thank God," she said, to my amazement. She leaned
towards me and said almost in a whisper, "I have been
praying to meet you for weeks now. I believe you are one of
the only people who can understand the desperate trouble
I'm in. Can I talk to you?" "Why, certainly," I said,
bewildered. After lunch she told me her story, and very sad
and terrible it was. She felt that my knowledge of the
Brethren would help in real understanding of a family
problem that had brought her right to the edge of despair
and breakdown. I felt deeply concerned for her, because I
did understand it, but I thought she herself needed the
church's ministry of healing to strengthen her in health, and
to give her some spiritual peace in dealing with it. So
together we went to Jean Coggan, whose loving care and
understanding helped so many clergy wives over the years.
As a result, a service of healing was arranged to take place
in the beautiful chapel at Scargill, and the resident chaplain
was happy to officiate. "I only want you and Jean there,"
the clergy wife said to me.

We all met quietly at the appointed time, and in the peace
and silence of that lovely place I looked out through the
great east window whose glass is plain, and saw the trees
and crags under the open sky. We knelt, and prayers were
said simply and earnestly. At the moment when healing of
mind and body was asked for my new friend, I remember
that everything else but her need was blotted out of my
mind. I felt so sad for her.

It was at that exact moment that something happened for
which it is almost impossible to find words. I must now
explain that for many years a tragic situation had existed in
my own family, and one of my two older half-sisters, unable
to tolerate my father's puritan faith, or his second marriage
to my mother, had caused terrible unhappiness in the family
to such an extent that even her own sister had, to my

mother's grief, broken off all relations with her for ever. My
mother had suffered a silent torture through all this, trying
desperately, endlessly, but unsuccessfully to put things right.
In time this very seriously affected her health. When my
sister had come home for very brief periods the unhappiness
was indescribable. It was a needless warfare, and total
misunderstanding. All my childhood days I had watched
my parents' sorrow, and saw my father's inflexible faith that
sustained him throughout the troubled and turbulent years.

When my sister eventually married a professor at London
University, a kind and delightful man on whom she lavished
all her pent-up love and emotion, we were glad for her, and
thankful she could find happiness in this way. My father
never showed anything but love and concern for her, and
perhaps this was to me the worst part of the situation. Being
something of a fighter, I wanted to cry out against her
misunderstanding of him and of my mother, go into battle
for justice and for my father's right to worship his Lord in
his own way in the small Biblical group, quite outside the
mainstream denominations, to which he belonged and
which she could not tolerate. Both sisters became dedicated
Anglicans, as devoted to their church as my father was to
his Brethren assembly. It was terrible that there was no
meeting-ground between them. When I left home I felt the
situation was best remedied by my keeping out of the way
for ever. I wished my sister well. After all, she had a very
attractive side, being intensely lively, intelligent, an able
scientist, and charming to her friends and occasionally even
to me. But I felt that really I was of no use or interest to her.
My parents' deep sorrow had been a slow heartbreak. I
wanted to try and forget it all.

As I could not bear to arouse the old violent antagonisms,
I was not willing for my husband and children to see
anything of her. I did nothing to cause any rift with her, but
simply faded silently out of her life. Sadness and bitterness
were locked up inside my mind, never to be expressed. I had
tried to forget my mother's suffering before her death, when
she lay, her brilliant mind clouded, begging for my sister's

forgiveness for anything she might have done wrong, and beseeching her to come to her. My sister did not come.

These sad matters of the past, part of the very fabric and pattern of my childhood and growing-up, could not have been further from my mind during the service of healing at Scargill that day.

Suddenly, while kneeling there, praying for my poor friend, my surroundings faded. I found myself, I do not know how, looking at a scene that I found both vivid and terrible. My sister was kneeling there, her arm flung across her face, and she was weeping bitterly, she whom I had never seen shed a tear in all the long years I had known her. So great was the grief I saw in her that I was wholly shattered. I found myself praying to our Lord to help her, saying, "I never knew she was so sad. How terrible this is. I can't stand such grief, Lord." And then, "Dear Lord, please help her, for I see now that our unhappiness was as nothing to hers."

Then I saw someone come slowly towards her, and put an arm around her shoulder as if to comfort her. I believed that Christ Himself had come to bring her His peace. But slowly, inexorably, I was made to look up at the figure standing in love beside her, and saw – myself.

It seemed an eternity before I returned to any consciousness of the chapel at Scargill. I found I was crying bitterly, and wanted to hide my face. I slowly realised that I, too, had experienced an amazing and unsought healing of the spirit, for all bitterness, resentment and sorrow were washed away for ever. I felt re-born, cleansed, renewed. It was so awesome a moment that at first I was dazed. Later I realised that much remained to be done.

My new life began when on my return home, I picked up the telephone and rang my sister's number near London. She was a widow now, living alone. Her astonishment at hearing my voice could hardly have been greater. I asked her if she would meet Cathy and me at the theatre in London the next week. She simply said, "Yes, I will."

We met as strangers. After all, thirty years had passed.

Nevertheless, the recognition was instant, and as we talked we found we had much in common. She was delighted that Tom was ordained, and soon David would be. We talked fast and endlessly, making up for the lost years. I saw how lonely she must have been, and I found that not only had my negative emotions of regret and sorrow, been wiped out, but I had been given a real insight into her sadness and misunderstandings. We both had, I think, our father's vitality, a fascinated interest in life, in people, in events. We were both enthusiastic for our own "thing". She was an ardent bell-ringer, I found, and as ceaselessly active as so many of my father's family were. So many of them were "alive" in a special way.

The day came to an end. It was the first of a number that we spent together. She became devoted to our family, Tom and David particularly. I shall always remember leaning out of the window of my carriage in the train before it left King's Cross for Newcastle, after that first meeting. In the twilight she stood beside the carriage door looking up at me, still talking animatedly. As the train drew out, dark against the yellowing evening sky, I saw her waving, waving, and knew that not only had I been healed but I had been given the inestimable privilege of being the healer of a broken relationship, for Christ had given me his own great gift of love.

Not long ago David took to her the last Sacrament of Holy Communion. "Thank you," she said to him, "for bringing Him to me." The next day she died.

11

"Just an ordinary Rev"

In his first year as a curate, Tom was now busy in the parish
and did a good deal of visiting. His knowledge of Ryton took
on a new depth as he became known in the homes of
parishioners. It was such a new rôle that it came freshly to
him. He even looked noticeably younger in this new life. He
came home each day and described in lively detail some of
the unusual places where he had been. His stories varied
from the faintly ridiculous which set us off laughing, to the
unusual or sad.

Walking up the front path of one house he was assaulted
by a ferocious dog, which rushed out from the back garden
and gave him a sharp bite on the leg before he could reach the
front door. When he did eventually knock, a lady opened the
door and eyed him coolly when he told her who he was. "Oh,
I'm not at all interested in heaven or church or anything like
that," she said frigidly. "I'm a member of the Communist
Party." "Well, your dog isn't very welcoming either," said
Tom. "It's just bitten my leg." However, her response was
not comradely, and he beat a tactical retreat, and came home
to bind up his wound.

He visited one lady whose only child, a teenage girl, was a

mongol. Like so many with this handicap, she was affectionate and had a real intelligence of a sort, and was anxious to
learn. Mother and daughter came to church every Sunday
morning, and it was plain the girl enjoyed the family
Communion service. After discussion with John Rowlands,
Tom went regularly for many weeks to prepare her for
Confirmation. "She understands a great deal," he told me,
"like what it means to be a friend of Jesus. She knows all
about giving and receiving presents, and she has grasped
what it means to receive the gift of love Jesus gives us, even
though we don't see Him. She understands about talking to
Jesus, and going to the special feast of Holy Communion to
which He has invited us." So steadily and gradually he taught
her something of what it means to follow Jesus, and to be
loved and wanted by Him. Her Confirmation was a
memorable day. Her face shone with joy. I used to see her and
her mother every Sunday morning afterwards, kneeling with
real devotion as they remembered our Lord and received the
bread and the wine as from Him. When over two years later
the time eventually came for us to leave Ryton, it was this girl
who stood in tears holding on to Tom's hand.

There were many homes where Tom enjoyed true warmth
and hospitality. He used to have interesting conversations
with all manner of people: the elderly doctor's widow, a
graduate, always up to date in current affairs and all the plays
in the Newcastle theatres, who had a quiet but deep and
sincere Christian faith; the elderly bachelor who was one of
the foremost authorities on making and playing the Northumbrian pipes; the couples whose marriages were threatening to
break up, or others who were hoping to be married in church
because "We want a white wedding". There were also those
who really had no conception of what Christianity is all
about: "I'm a good-living man, sir, and don't harm anyone";
and those who never saw any point in the church at all
because: "I don't like the people who go to church, anyway.
I'd far rather worship God when I'm walking in the country."
And there were always those who never had any time: "I'm
afraid I don't come to church. You see I have to do my laundry
on Sundays, as I'm out at work all week." Or, "Well, no, I'm

not really interested in religion. We always go out in the country on Sundays, and we have to wash the car in the mornings."

Gradually, however, he seemed to get through to a number of people who grew to trust him, and one thing interested me: his reputation as a good solicitor seemed to make people respect him, and appreciate that he knew well the ways of the world, and in their eyes had, therefore, a deeper understanding of the man in the pew and the non-churchgoer than many parsons. Because of this, people often came to him with problems that they clearly believed could be solved by his skill as a professional man, as well as by his position as an ordained minister of the church.

A year later he was ordained priest in Durham Cathederal. The Call which had unexpectedly come to him years earlier was now wholly confirmed.

The months passed. Winter came early and the weather grew very cold. Roads sparkled with frost and were covered with patches of treacherous black ice. The air was sharp and cut the face, and the trees, whose last few dead leaves hung grey and stiff with rime, stood black and skeletal against the pale cold sky.

By now I had joined the rota as a driver for the Meals on Wheels Service in the district, which was excellently organised. We worked in pairs fetching the meals from the kitchens at the huge nearby Stella Power Station, and carrying them in the car in a big "Hotlock" container. Some of the homes we visited were chilly and depressing as the winter bit deeper. Tiny ineffective fires burned in the grates of small, dark, damp rooms, where lonely, housebound, elderly people waited expectantly for their hot meal. Some of the saddest were old men, often widowers, who lived in dirty rooms where the hearth was never cleaned and was full of dead grey ash and burnt-out bits of coal, and thick dust lay everywhere. It was often hard to find a space on the table on which to put down the hot meal, for there was a clutter of dirty cups and plates, unwashed for several days. Yet other houses were sparkling and bright. Everything was polished until it shone, and often there were colourful pot plants and many photos of children and grandchildren. Little old ladies with advanced arthritis hobbled cheerfully around, somehow keeping their homes fresh and attractive. They were always waiting happily and expectantly for the treat of a hot meal prepared and cooked for them.

One rather gloomy small terrace house was always silent even when we knocked on the door, which had always been left just ajar for us. But inside, in the back room off a dark hall, a little old lady was always waiting for us. Although she was deaf and rarely heard our knock, she would be standing there expectantly, as if she was straining to catch the faintest sound of movement. Always she would smile brilliantly at us. She wore a dark blue woolly cap, for her house was chilly, and a shabby shawl was drawn round her shoulders. As we uncovered the hot dishes, searching in her kitchenette for plates to put the food on, she would gaze and gaze at what we had brought. We would help her to the table and ease her onto the chair. "How lovely! Roast meat *and* apple pie! Oh my! I am going to enjoy it." We knew that the meals brought to her twice a week were the only good food she had. Before we went out to go to the next person on our round, she would grip our hands as if she could not bear to let us go. One day the sweet welcoming smile we had grown to expect, turned to tears. "It's so *good* to see you," she said. "The days are so long and my feet pain me dreadfully. I've spoken to no one for a week." Audrey, my rota partner, put her arm around the thin shoulders. It seemed so sad to leave her there. Not long afterwards she was taken away to hospital. We never saw her again. There was poverty and sadness on Tyneside, and many gaps that the welfare state could not fill, yet there was so much rugged and sturdy courage to be seen in the people.

Life in the parish certainly was very varied, and was not without its drama, in the real meaning of the word. "Let's have a religious drama club," some of us had said blithely, when a fairly new member of the congregation turned out to be an expert, trained at the Royal Academy of Dramatic Art. After thinking over our idea, she had nobly volunteered to produce a play in the church. Ventures such as this are not all plain sailing, but if you are prepared to be frustrated, maddened, exhausted, and in the end stimulated and inspired, then it is an activity I can recommend.

Our producer decided to attempt Christopher Fry's play, *The Boy with the Cart,* the story of a Saxon peasant boy, who, for love of God, determines in face of impossible difficulties to build a church. In the large cast, Tom, Chris, Cathy and I all had parts. In our rehearsals we languished and froze in the unheated church building. We could not remember our lines. But we battled away, going over the scenes again and again. Everyone lent a hand at some task, like the ladies who dyed old sheets for willing helpers to transform into colourful costumes. Slowly the play took shape and gradually we were caught up with the beauty of the words. When the actual performance took place it seemed like a miracle, for the cast, drawn from every church in Ryton and from every walk of life, found that the play had suddenly come alive.

It so happened that I had asked the head of the boys' approved school, where I went frequently, if he would like a party of boys to come over to the performance. He was glad to send quite a number. After the play was over, we gathered around to usher the boys back into their minibus. To the boys' extreme pleasure the engine would not start. In the ensuing excitement, several of us deployed ourselves to keep a sharp eye open for would-be absconders for the boys seemed to be putting their heads together in a suspicious way, to plan an escape I guessed, while the master peered into the engine. He was unable to get a spark of life out of it, so at last a few of us took three or four boys each in our own cars, to drive them back to the school. In fact six piled into ours, chattering animatedly about the play. "Miss, that wind was good!" It was indeed. The powerful sound-recording, graduating from breeze upwards, had accidentally hit "Hurricane", filling the church with an apocalyptic blast of sound, and drowning all the actors' voices. "Miss, was that old man yer 'usband?" another asked. One of the most memorable performances of the evening had been Tom's. With the help of a theatrical wig he had appeared as a remarkable and venerable figure, with long grey hair onto his shoulders, and he had removed his few false teeth for verisimilitude. (For reasons not then entirely plain to me, this proved to be one of the most successful acts of his ministry! "I do so admire a man of your husband's talents who is willing to let his hair down," one lady said to me, but I know she was really alluding to the teeth! It certainly humanised him in the eyes of the people of Ryton.) "Yes, that was my husband," I said to the boy, wondering what age he must think we were. "Miss, is 'e a Rev?" "Well, yes." "What sort of a Rev, Miss? A Bishop?" I suddenly choked, not only because of the overpowering fumes of spearmint being breathed down my neck. "No. Just an ordinary Rev. He's a curate actually."

A warm and sympathetic pause indicated that there was no need to be cast down by life's little disappointments, and presently a very husky and encouraging voice said from behind my ear: "'E's just a Rev that sort of 'elps another Rev, then?" I nodded, without comment. It was a good description.

I briskly marched my six friendly potential absconders into the school, and as they waved goodbye and disappeared down the corridor, a loud voice was heard reiterating: "That wind was *dead* good."

Yes, religious drama had its points.

The winter days passed, and soon the Christmas decorations appeared in the big shops in Newcastle. About this time Cathy had to go into hospital. She had fallen on a sharp outcrop of rock on the moors near the farm some weeks previously and was clearly in a good deal of pain. The doctor could find nothing wrong with her except heavy bruising, and in her usual cheerful way she insisted on playing hockey and living a normal life, although I noticed she limped sometimes. Occasionally she said, "My knee is really bad." Then she had to be in bed with a feverish cold, and when she was better found her knee had completely stiffened up. She could not bend it. Our doctor then sent her to the big university teaching hospital, the Royal Victoria Infirmary, in Newcastle, for X-rays, and an examination by a senior orthopaedic surgeon. We were shocked to learn it was not a trivial injury: she had a partially severed tendon in the knee and must be operated on immediately, as otherwise there was a strong possibility she would be severely crippled later on.

Cathy, who is now a state registered nurse, had loved hospitals and anything medical since she was four years old, when she had gazed at the lifelike tableau of the dying Nelson on the *Victory* in Madame Tussaud's, with a bowl of apparently blood-stained water beside him, and the ship's surgeon attempting to staunch his wound. "Oh *poor* Nelson," she had said. "I do wish I had been there to help him." We could not move her from the scene, and in the end she had to be forcibly carried away. Ever since then, occasions when the boys had nose bleeds or little wounds delighted her. She would rush off and appear with bowls of water and cotton wool, and eagerly mop them up. Now the operation seemed to have no terrors for her and she went into hospital smiling happily as if going to a party.

In the event, the operation must have been quite an ordeal. Afterwards she had to be put into a heavy plaster from the ankle right to the top of the leg, and for some days she had a great deal of pain and was unable to move about. But she never complained and was always smiling when I went each day to the orthopaedic ward to visit her. The plaster had to stay on for six weeks and she would need crutches, we learned. When I saw some of the children in the other beds, some with severe and even tragic cases of spinal deformity, withered legs, twisted feet, I realised what burdens some parents were carrying. Rosy, a lively enchanting child of about eleven, lay in the bed opposite Cathy. One of her legs, withered and severely shrunk after polio, was held in a kind of sling which was suspended from the ceiling, and a thin shiny steel rod was fixed right through the leg from front to back connected to the sling. It looked horrifying. Rosy was, therefore, effectively immobilised and was a long-stay patient. How could a child endure it, I wondered. But she was the life and soul of the ward, full of laughter, and always cheering and encouraging any younger children when their pain was bad. She came from the dreary and notorious Scotswood Road area, from one of the poor houses which had not then been demolished. It was a place where the police patrol in pairs and crime is

rife. Each evening her large jolly mother puffed up the stairs
to the ward, after taking two bus journeys to come. She always
wore a grey headscarf and a shabby, dark coat stretched
across her full figure. She would bring tiny gifts for Rosy,
unpacking them from an old shopping bag, and Rosy would
exclaim happily over everything she brought. The two
seemed so happy to be together, you would imagine they had
not a care in the world.

One evening as we left the ward, Rosy's mother told me
her story. Like many women living in that gloomy district,
she had a very large family in which Rosy was the second
eldest. She obviously loved them all, with an abundantly
generous nature. But the father was unemployed. Things
were very hard indeed, there were so many little children to
feed and clothe and care for. Shoes were so expensive, but of
course there were always the jumble sales. She smiled kindly
at me as she talked, her pity flowing out to Cathy who she
thought was "a canny brave lass". Then she said, "How
lovely for her to come home for Christmas." She talked so
cheerfully of her difficulties that I felt privileged to be with
her. "Of course, none of us can have any Christmas this
year," she went on. "You see we've saved up every spare
penny we've got for Rosy. It's to be her Christmas this year.
Don't tell her. It's a secret. We've bought her – a WATCH!"
Her eyes shone. She was full of pleasure because all the
family had agreed to this, and they knew there could be no
toys, no new clothes, no treats, no special Christmas fare for
them. "But it's Rosy getting better, that's all that matters this
year," she said. Tentatively, I asked her where she lived,
thinking up an excuse. "Cathy would like to send a card to
Rosy," I explained.

When I got back to Ryton, I spoke to my friends in our
coffee group. We had met for years once a week in term time
while our children were growing up, at first just for pleasure,
and then together we had undertaken a varied number of
schemes for different charities and also for Christian projects.
Now I told them about Rosy's family and the children who
could have no Christmas. I knew they would respond. Within
a few days there were two or three big cardboard grocery

boxes full of toys, children's books, clothes, crackers, sweets, a Christmas pudding and enough food for a family Christmas dinner.

It was a dark cold evening just before Christmas when a friend and I drove down to the Scotswood Road area. The streets were dreary, the terraced houses mean and shabby. Some windows were lit up by the lights on little artificial Christmas trees, with a few strands of tinsel on them. But Rosy's house was dark. I knocked, and at last there were running children's steps, and the door opened cautiously a few inches. Several rather tousled little heads appeared clustered together, and then like a mother hen sweeping her chicks aside, Rosy's mother stood in the dark doorway. "Please will you accept these things for the children from Father Christmas," I said awkwardly, handing in the boxes. She stood there, silent for once, as if turned to stone. Then she looked at us beaming through tears, clasping one of the boxes to her chest. "Happy Christmas," we said. "Have a really happy Christmas, and give Cathy's love to Rosy."

We got hastily into the car and, not speaking, drove fast out of Newcastle, back to Ryton and our warm bright homes, full of pretty Christmas decorations and presents waiting for every member of the family.

For a time we were stricken, somehow.

On the Friday before Christmas Tom and Chris and I walked through the cold, frosty air down to the old village. We saw groups of elderly women stumbling down the icy footpath across the village green, passing like animated silhouettes across the floodlit white front of the Cross Inn, whose windows glowed with a warm orange light. The men followed behind, mufflers swathed high round their necks, shouting jocular remarks to each other. They passed the old stone cross where Wesley once preached, and made their way to the Victorian church hall on the far side of the green. They were followed by groups of children, jumping and shouting and sliding on the thin powdery snow which had just dusted the roads. Families followed, and many other people from the village. Breath came out in little clouds drifting in the frosty air, as everyone made their way into the hall.

Inside there was a transformation. The shabbiness of the walls was softened in the mellow flickering light of dozens of brightly-coloured candles, placed on the windowsills among the holly and the evergreens, and between the red and silver decorations on the small tables which stood around the room. All harsh outlines were hidden, and faces seemed softly glowing and transformed, like portraits in a Dutch masterpiece.

Everyone sat down around the tables, where cups and saucers and plates of biscuits hinted at the refreshments to come for the singers, for this was the annual night of Carols by Candlelight, the best night of the year, some said, when young and old from every sort of home and occupation in the parish gathered together to welcome Christmas.

"Well, Andy, in good voice? Lend a hand with the chairs there, Dickie. Now, choir, gather up here in front of everyone where you can be seen, and we'll be off." Our rector, who still had something of the military man about him after his wartime service in the Western Desert as Army chaplain, gathered up his troops, briefly harangued them and deployed them for action. Then, raising his hand, he announced the first carol, "Hark! The Herald Angels Sing".

The burst of singing drowned the tinny sound of the old piano as the sturdy Durham men and women from pit and factory, from homes and industry, sang as only they knew how. Gnarled hands, roughened and scarred hands, hands that had handled pick and shovel, old hands that had wielded the posse stick in the laundry tub, spontaneously tapped out the rhythm on the tables, beside the smooth hands of the younger men and women, the white-collar workers, and the children. It was a joyous harmony, for we were a community where everyone was welcomed, and sorrows and hardships could be eased for a brief space.

"Happy Christmas, Rev," I said under my breath as I looked at Tom singing happily, with his fine voice echoing out true and clear. "It's a good life."

12

A Cry of Children

Tom and I were both involved with work with young delinquents, quite apart from work with his youth club during his curacy at Ryton. Coincidentally he had been appointed a manager of an approved school for girls, and I for one for boys. Both schools are now, of course, known as community homes.

Just as a moving picture passes across a lighted screen, so a stream of children flash across the memory, and I see them again as if it were yesterday. So often there was little one could do for them, but the questions their lives posed remain uncomfortably in the mind.

I was watching Mary in the juvenile court. She was small with pretty, delicate features in a pale delicate face, and bright brown wavy hair that fell in a cloud about her shoulders. She stood there, painfully afraid, with a mute appeal in her eyes. She had been brought before the magistrates for a series of thefts from some of the big shops in Newcastle city centre shortly before Christmas. The case was presented by the police; and the chairman of the bench, a firm woman with keen insight and understanding, was unusually gentle with her. The plea was guilty. When the case had been heard, and the witnesses had left the stand, Mary was taken forward to speak to the chairman, who quietly questioned her. With the papers about her before them, the justices conferred.

Mary had come from a very poor home, they found; she was the eldest of a large family, and she was twelve years old. Her father was mortally ill, and her mother was a sick woman unable to do much, and Mary looked after all the little ones. Shortly before Christmas she realised that in her home on Christmas morning there would be no toys at all for her little brothers and sisters whom she loved with a fierce passion. The decorations were all up in her school, the shops were glittering with beautiful things, and the other children were talking about the presents they were going to get. In her despair Mary decided that she alone must be Father Christmas. She had no money, and had never stolen before. But now surely it could not be all that wrong – just for the kids' sake. So one Saturday morning she slipped into the city and went into the brightly-lit stores, dazzled by the display of beautiful things, such as she had never possessed. She secretly slipped toys for her little brothers and sisters into carrier bags. She took nothing at all for herself. She had not been able to bear the thought of their disappointment on Christmas Day. Mary was seen by a store detective, and brought before the court. Now she was in despair because the lovely bright new toys had all been taken away, and in her ignorance she thought she might be sent to prison. If so, she knew there was no one else to look after the little family and to help her mother.

After a few moments, the justices announced their decision. Mary was put on probation, and in that moment she found a new friend. For the probation officer went to work at once, and the whole sad family became her concern.

A big box of toys arrived for Christmas, and new hope came into a pathetic child's life.

I shall not forget Jonathan easily. He stood in the juvenile court, silent, pale and totally withdrawn, looking into some distant place far away as if he was not with us at all. He was neatly dressed, with short, carefully-brushed hair. He was fourteen. He could hardly be persuaded to answer any of the questions put to him and when he did his voice was a thin whisper. He, too, was accused of theft: pens, pencils and torches, small objects, from the shop in the street where he lived. But why? We learned his story.

Abandoned at birth, Jonathan had passed from one children's home to another, fitting in nowhere. Fostering had failed, no one could get through to him. He could make no personal relationships, and now he was virtually unplaceable. Nobody wanted him or loved him. He had become a totally institutionalised child. But why the thefts? It seemed that at school he had not got the little ordinary things the other children automatically had, crayons, pencils, a pen. He decided he must get them for himself in order to be like the other children, because no one must guess how unwanted he was. Jonathan had become incapable of emotion, a broken unloved child with no future. He was put on probation, but his future was bleak.

It was at the boys' approved school that my work brought me into contact with fair-haired Tim. He was thirteen, hard, tough, restless, uncaring. He looked at me coldly and with dislike from large blue eyes. After a time I learned he had one great interest; he collected foreign stamps. I realised he had a much higher I.Q. than most of the boys. I told him I would bring him some stamps one day. It was a breakthrough. His eyes shone. He became animated. He began to chat to me whenever I chanced to see him. Eventually I put some interesting stamps in an envelope and handed them to him one day when I met him just coming in from the grounds outside. He opened the envelope with intense pleasure and examined them carefully. Suddenly he looked up, and a shadow crossed his face. "Miss," he said, "can I ask you something?" "Yes, of course." "I'm due home for a weekend soon, Miss, and I don't know where I'm to go." "How's that then, Tim?" "Miss –" he paused, unable to go on. I saw his face crumple. He bent his head, and stuffed his knuckles into his eyes, and was shaken by sobs. I put my hand on his shoulder. "Tell me then, Tim." "Miss, my mum and dad have split up. I don't know where I'm going. I don't know who I belong to any more." He sobbed again. His grief seemed to be tearing him apart, and there was little I could do but just stand there and let him cry.

Tim was one of the many thousands of children in our country whose life has fallen apart. He had turned to crime when he saw the threatening cracks in his home life. His behaviour then had been a cry for help. It had gone unheeded. With the final loss of a settled home I had little doubt he would probably turn to more serious crime, for he felt no one cared, and somehow he had to hit back at a cruel world.

Paul was a worse problem; totally disruptive, aggressive, a born troublemaker. He could make life atrocious for the hard-working staff at the approved school, and could set a whole class of boys in a ferment, and cause a violent disturbance, and then he would run amok, smashing everything in his way. One morning when I went in, I found the staff who had been working to calm him down were exhausted and, in any case, needed to give time to the other boys on whom Paul's behaviour was having a dreadful effect, causing them to be very disruptive too. "Well, I don't mind talking to him for a bit," I said. "Perhaps a stranger can draw his fire." I had never met Paul, and was, in fact, curious to see what he was like.

I sat in the common room and presently there was the sound of a struggle, and Paul was pushed inside the door by a master. I looked at him with astonishment. He was so tiny for thirteen years, more like a ten-year-old. Could this little lad really have caused such trouble? His hair was dust-coloured, and stuck up in a sort of rough crew-cut all over his head. He was very pale, very hostile and very sullen. He eyed me like a wild animal that might spring at any minute. "Sit down, Paul," I said pointing to a chair. Slowly he did so, and we looked at each other. "You've had a bad morning then," I said. A long silence. "Well, you see I don't know you at all, and you don't know me, so I'd like to hear about you. Have you a big family?" His head lifted then, and a fleeting expression came into the blank eyes. I could not tell what it meant. An answer came slowly at last. "Yes, there's twelve of us kids." "Twelve! Well that's a fine big family. Do you get on with them? I expect you're missing them." "No, I'm not. I hate them." "Paul, why? You can't hate them all." At all costs I felt I must get him to talk. At last he said with his face hidden again, "'Cos they all hate me." "Well I'm sure they don't," I said, "but if you carry on like this morning, it's not surprising. No one enjoys that. It makes everyone angry. But there's more to it than that I'm sure, isn't there?"

Paul bent forward, and rocked to and fro. "They do hate me. They don't want me. No one in my family has ever been to see me here. Everyone else has visitors. No one comes for me – ever." Slowly hard tears trickled down the grubby face. We sat there in silence. "How long have you been here?" "A year." What *could* one do? Nothing really. I imagined he must have been home sometime during that period, but I also knew that almost all the other boys had some visitor at intervals who brought them comics and little gifts. Relatives generally came from time to time even from the worst homes.

"Paul, do you like chocolates?" His head lifted, the expression incredulous, a glimmer of hope in the eyes. "Because if you really try to do better for the next month, I'll bring you a box of chocs. That's a promise, but it's up to you. I shall ask the masters to give me a report." I said this because I saw that no one had ever brought him anything. His family were glad to get rid of him, one less mouth to feed, one nuisance out of the way. Let the State look after him. They did not care. But if perhaps one person showed a little interest, brought him something, he might respond. Was it a forlorn hope, I wondered?

"What do you want to do when you leave school, Paul?" "Go in the Army, Miss." "Well, they won't have you like this. A pity because you might make a good soldier. See what you can do about it." He went to the door, gave me a long look and went out quietly.

The following month I learned from the staff that he had improved a little, and things were rather better. Solemnly I handed him a parcel. He could hardly believe it; a brilliant smile lit up his plain little face. He hugged it, and rushed off, jumping and leaping down the corridor. Nevertheless I could see little hope for his future, once he left the school.

Were these children, typical of so many, more sinned against than sinning? Very often. The hard core of brutality and violence in some of them was, however, an appallingly difficult and evil thing to deal with, and I often felt the staff did a heroic job, and it seemed wonderful when there were successes.

This work posed many questions. What could the church, the Christian community, do for children in this situation? Tom and I often discussed this, for he found that the girls at the approved school were in some ways an even worse problem than the boys. Often absconding, wild tearaways, sometimes violent, hysterical and destructive, they were in constant danger from any men who might exploit them. They spent much time tattooing themselves with ink, boot polish and needles. At times they made themselves look horrific, yet their one wish was to find a man, get married and have a home. They had a basic insecurity, and so often came from broken homes; for behind their anti-social behaviour there was so often the same tragic background as that of many of the boys.

I talked frequently with the Head of the boys' school. He was a youngish man of great character, blunt, fearless, with enormous energy and insight, and a dynamic, forward-looking approach to his work. I grew to believe he was, at heart, an extremely kind, sensitive man. He used to tell me

that he was an agnostic, yet questioned me with great
sensitivity about Tom's ordination. In some respects I grew
to feel he was one of the most Christian people in outlook
that I knew. He had grown up in an evangelical Christian
home; his father was an elderly Pentecostal minister who
had had a wonderfully dramatic conversion while working
at the pits in Wales. "My father prays for me every day," he
told me. "Perhaps he'll get me converted in the end!" He
had, clearly, a deep affection and respect for his father.

He was much embittered by a local Anglican church, for
on various occasions he arranged for a group of boys to
attend the morning service there, accompanied by masters.
But the respectable congregation had complained. They did
not want boys like that there. It had been made very plain
that they were not welcome. I burned with shame. "Well,
the Methodists take them," he told me, "good honest folk,
they're willing to have them." Sometimes he raged about
outsiders' attitudes to his boys, for whose welfare he was
deeply concerned. "The State looks after their bodies, but it
doesn't give a damn for their souls," he said, adding
despairingly, "nor does the established church, it seems."

Tom and I were very concerned. Tom talked to John
Rowlands, always a good and understanding friend. It was
agreed that if the Head cared to send any of the boys over
to our church at Ryton at any time, they would be made
welcome. After that a group quite often came to Evensong
with a master, and we made a point of talking to them and
making them feel welcome afterwards. In general their
behaviour was good, but then I always found that most of
them responded strongly and positively to kindness and
courtesy.

It was the Head's wife, whose life was almost impossibly
busy, who volunteered to drive over to help at the youth
club Tom started at this time at Ryton. Over the years she
and her husband became valued friends.

As I look back on that work with which we got so deeply
involved, I think perhaps above all of the father of this

Headmaster, the elderly Pentecostal minister, who came to stay at the school with his son from time to time.

Whenever he came he went to meet the boys, many of them extremely disturbed, and some having committed sickening and violent crimes. He would gather them round, and ask who would join him in a prayer-meeting that night. The response was dramatic and unbelievable. Large numbers would forego their favourite leisure activity – outdoor sport or athletics, or swimming or whatever it might be – just to be with him. At the prayer-meeting they would crowd around him as he prayed for them. "There they kneel," said the Head, "getting converted, some of them again and again, weeping sometimes, tears of repentance. Oh yes, they'll forget, most of them, until the next time he comes, but they always go back to him. Perhaps something sticks. A memory of someone who once really loved them. Who knows?"

I see him still, that gentle little old man, an easy target for muggers, you might think, but with a lion-hearted courage, and a total unswerving faith, who held out his arms in love to those desperately lost boys. They, feeling that love, knelt around him, pressed close to get near him, and listened while he prayed for every one of them. He told them of a mighty Saviour who loved them with an everlasting love, who was ready to forgive all the wrong they had ever done; for He came to die for them, and to blot out all their sins; to redeem them and to bring them salvation and new life. For, he told them, Christ Jesus had said that he came not to call the righteous, but sinners to repentance. In his agony on the Cross, had He not turned to a dying and repentant thief and said, "Today shalt thou be with me in Paradise"?

13

"The Killer"

During Tom's second year as a curate at Ryton he had grown concerned for the younger teenagers in the area, a few of whom came to the church with their parents, but the majority of whom roamed the streets at night. After consulting with John Rowlands, he got permission to start a youth club for them on Sunday nights in the church hall. Here he spent the whole of each Sunday evening after the church service getting to know the girls and boys, and trying, often vainly, to induce them to take part in various creative activities. He used to come home pale and completely exhausted. "I can't *think* why they come, it's just a rabble," he often said, "but they say they actually enjoy it!" Accompanied by Noël, a young Methodist schoolmaster who was the only person to volunteer to help him, he battled on. The difficulties were enormous. Eventually two or three young wives and I said we, too, would go down and work as helpers at the club. The experience was memorable, and that was how I came to meet Kevin.

Rushing down the stone cellar stairs, he rounded the bend at the bottom and took the last steps in a flying leap, and suddenly saw me standing there. Glaring myopically through the thick lenses of his glasses, his face only about two feet from mine, he stood poised like a coiled spring, his short red hair sticking straight up from his head as if somehow the law of gravity was reversed and was pulling it upwards. Its colour was so vivid that it looked as if it might spark alight with some hidden electric force. A second passed, and suddenly he clasped both hands hard around my neck and shouted, "I'm a killer."

At such moments one seeks for some inner instinctive wisdom. "That's going to be a bit unfortunate for both of us then," I said lightly. The tense freckled face relaxed, and the eyes, wary now, sought mine questioningly, and suddenly he laughed, and loosed his hands and silently followed me into the dimly-lit room, where two cheerful and long-suffering housewives were dispensing squash and crisps from a battered trestle table, while an old tea urn bubbled in the corner.

The walls of this room were a dismal green. On the shabby wooden floor a few shabby chairs stood forlornly. A single unshaded light bulb swung to and fro where it hung from the ceiling, as twenty or more teenagers stamped and rocked and shouted and yelled, and gulped and crunched and spat. Upstairs in the large church hall the sounds of shouts, thuds, running feet and crashes, proclaimed that the parish church youth club this Sunday evening was running normally.

I left the refreshments, being on patrol duty upstairs that night, and went to do the rounds with the huge muzzled Old English sheepdog, brought by one of our helpers, who proved one of our best allies against incipient violence. There were rumours that a gang from the city was coming out to break up the club that evening. The district around and outside Ryton was, of course, what sociologists term a disadvantaged area of high unemployment and much delinquency, where parents who passed the dreary hours at clubs and pubs locked their children out of their houses so that they would not smash up each others' dwellings – they could hardly be called homes. I stopped with the dog at the various activity points, chatting with those playing chess, snakes and ladders, draughts and other games at small tables, and went on to the carpentry corner where the excessively happy and boisterous activity with bits of scrap wood was, I suddenly realised, turning into the preparation of a weaponry, as rough but dangerous swords, daggers and truncheons were being rather secretively fashioned. Noël, the volunteer helper, who regularly gave up his Sunday evenings to assist Tom in what many felt was a forlorn project doomed to hopeless failure, had tumbled to this too, I saw. "They'll murder each other before the night's out," I said to him under my breath as I passed.

A little later I suddenly noticed "the killer" again. This was his first visit to the club, and he was sitting so quietly on a bench that it seemed sinister until I realised he was straining intently to read through a pile of old comics, and he was lost to the world. Under the light I saw that he looked about fourteen, was hard and stocky, surprisingly neat, and cleaner than most. He was well turned out in a blue anorak and grey trousers. "Someone's got a good mum," I thought.

The evening was like most club nights, exhausting for the helpers, apparently surprisingly satisfactory for the kids. They scuffled and whispered and giggled through Tom's five minute epilogue at the end, except for the two or three who listened and were oddly attentive. When it ended, and they eventually all rushed out yelling, "the killer" passed me shouting as loud as any of them, "I'm coming back next Sunday, and I want some more of them comics."

The weeks passed. Tom wrestled valiantly with his unruly toughs and the strident, bright-eyed girls. Fearful problems arose regularly. The ill-lit passages downstairs near the lavatories had to be constantly, unceasingly patrolled. We did it on a rota basis. Illicit beer was brought in one night by two wild fourteen-year-olds, and they were quickly barred outside the club for that night. Their anguished knockings at the outer doors sounded as if we were being besieged. The city gang did turn up one dark night just as the club was over, and the girls were leaving to go home. They catapulted back inside falling over each other, screaming in real terror. In this moment of crisis I advanced outside with the dog and looked at a sullen mob waiting under the street light with menacing appearance. Providentially – and I really felt this to be so – I recognised the hulking bully leading them. I happened to know his mother. I found myself advancing upon them and smiling, and saying, "Why, Gary, it's you! How's your mum these days?" So great was the shock to him of this warm reception that he muttered something, and turned and drifted away into the darkness followed by his bewildered and sullen cohorts.

On another night the Archdeacon of Durham came to preach in our beautiful twelfth-century church to a large congregation. The service had already begun when we became uneasily aware that the back pews were occupied by a number of strange recumbent forms, apparently asleep. Their dirty jeans, cropped heads and large "bovver" boots proclaimed their origin. They were, surprisingly, totally silent during the service, and remained prostrate, but as they herded out at the end, they said aggressively, "We've been to church, so now we're coming to the club."

Sadly the club had eventually to be disbanded. The hall structure was suffering, and the behaviour of a minority was totally destructive. Yet it was these same boys who came to our home and begged us to start a craft club for them. "We wouldn't be bad in your home, Miss," they said. "No one else wants us." This was hardly surprising, I told them. Eventually two talented volunteer helpers came and took on twelve boys, including "the killer", and they met each week in the boxroom that had been Tom's quiet study at the end of our house. Miracles were worked as the boys were helped to construct a model of our own village, whose old houses remained unspoilt, although council estates and industrial development surrounded and almost threatened to engulf it. Most of the boys had never created anything before and now saw with wonder something develop by the new skill of their own hands. I promised I would ask if the model village, its church and houses illuminated by tiny torch lights, could be put on a table at the back of the church for all to see at Christmas, which was now getting very near.

We were slowly getting to know a little more about the lives of "our boys". At least half of them were on probation. "The killer" told us nothing, ever, although at last we learned that his name was Kevin. He had become entirely hooked on making beautiful red crêpe paper flowers for Christmas decorations, a skill taught him by a kind and gifted friend of ours who visited the club once or twice. Under her guidance he worked feverishly, silently. He wanted to take some flowers home for Christmas, he said.

It was a Monday when a police officer came to our house. "I hear Kevin Black* comes here regularly," he said with apparent disapproval. "Is he here?" "Certainly he comes to a small craft club, but he is not here – why?" "He's disappeared again, that's all. It's always happening. He's been missing a week now," said the officer. "Isn't his mother very anxious then?" I said. "His *mother*! He's got no mother. He just lives in the children's home up the road." A picture formed in my mind. Those neat clothes, that trim haircut. Yes, it added up. I said that if there was any news I would let the police know, and meanwhile I would phone the home at once.

The voice at the other end of the line chattered and clacked. "Such a trouble, so ungrateful, so thoughtless. We do all we can. I can't do more. There's the others to think of. But he loves that club at your house. Talks of nothing else. No, his mother went off five years ago, leaving the five boys. They're all separated now. The older ones are in trouble, Borstal and that. No, there's no father now. Kevin was supposed to be going home to him this Christmas, and was *most* excited. His father was going to make a home for him and his younger brother, or so he *said*. I didn't believe him. I'd heard it too often before." "Well, what happened?" I asked. "Oh, the father. Oh! – very unfortunate, that. He dropped dead a week ago. Kevin cried, then the shutters

*Kevin Black is not, of course, the real name of the boy in this true story

came down. He hasn't spoken about it since. He's very hard, you know."

I felt stunned and hung up the phone. Outside it was sleeting. There were icicles of freezing rain, and the pavements were dark and wet. It was getting relentlessly colder. I phoned my friend who had taught Kevin to make the decorations. She was touched and fascinated because he had worked so compulsively, never lifting his head from his work. Now she was distressed. "I must try and find him," I said. "I'll keep in touch. I'm going out in the car to look for him." It was growing dark. I drove through the furthest housing estates where paper and rubbish swirled in the windy streets, down past the power station, into cul-de-sacs, through narrow streets. It was hopeless, of course. So I drove slowly back past the old church, and there I suddenly saw a group of shabby figures furtively running out of reach of the car's probing headlights. Quickly I drew up beside them. It was "our boys" and instinctively I guessed they knew where Kevin was. They looked blank. "We don't know, Miss, he's gone." I did not believe them, and suddenly saw a boy at the back of the group with a scarf over his face slip quickly away into the darkness. I was sure it was Kevin. I put down the car window and called to him, but the others came crowding round as if to hide him. "He's so miserable, Miss. He's been sleeping out for a week. We've been bringing him food. He hates it at that home." "Where's he been sleeping?" "In a hole in the wall near the church, Miss. We'll show you." "In this bitter weather! I just don't believe you." "It's *true*. We brought him a blanket to keep him warm, and we steal bits of bread from our homes for him, and cold potatoes too." They looked at me pleadingly.

Unbelievably, it proved indeed to be true. They showed me a deep hollow space in a broken-down wall at the edge of the churchyard. A tiny pile of clothes and a filthy blanket lay inside it, and a bag of cold potatoes and some stale sliced bread.

I went back and sat in the car and called to Kevin in the darkness. "How would you like a drive in the car?" Slowly, agonisingly slowly, he came to the window, the scarf still over his face, only his eyes, cold and dead, showing. "I'm not going back to that home," he said. "All right, I won't take you back unless you agree," I said. "But how would you like to come and see my friend who taught you to make those lovely flowers?" Now his eyes showed a fleeting emotion. Very slowly, he opened the passenger door and climbed into the car, shivering violently and coughing. "I think you'd better have some coffee and sandwiches at my home first," I said.

He stood with Tom and me in our kitchen, withdrawn, empty of all emotion, it seemed, gulping the hot coffee and eating large sandwiches voraciously. I slipped out and phoned my friend, and she, kind as ever, began to prepare a special welcome for him, for she was delighted to hear that he was safe, but shocked at his story. It was a wonder he was not seriously ill after sleeping out in the bitter weather.

We drove through the dark night for seven miles and at last arrived, and walked up the path to her front door. There was a Christmas garland hanging on it in welcome, with bright red and gold ribbons. Kevin gazed astonished. The door opened and our friend held out her hands to Kevin and drew him into the light and warmth. It was a beautiful home, full of costly antiques and objets d'art, and deep, comfortable chairs and sofas. Big fires glowed. Wonderful decorations filled the house and sparkled and shone. Kevin stood and gazed and gazed around in wonder. Then he was given a big plate of sausage rolls and mince pies and made to sit on the floor by the blazing fire. I think then he must have felt he had come into some strange paradise, but I sensed strongly that he knew all too well that he was only a stranger in it. Presently I left him and went into the kitchen where my friend was cutting him some cake. She looked up and her eyes were full of tears. "I can't bear it," she said. "Our children have everything. He has nothing. What can we do?" "I have an idea that he might go back to the home if he had the materials to make more paper flowers for the children there," I said. She went immediately and brought a boxful of brightly coloured crêpe and silver paper, and went and sat on the floor beside him. His eyes suddenly shone.

"Can I make some more of them flowers for the Home?" he asked. Then, to my astonishment, he added desperately, turning to me, "but if I go back, can I come to the Christmas midnight service at church, and see the model village and my flowers and everything?" "I'll do all I can to arrange that," I said, praying inwardly that the people at the Home would allow him to come.

It was time to go. He seized his box, hugging it closely to his side, and we went out onto the front door step. At first he said nothing, then suddenly he turned and put up his face to be kissed in so natural and spontaneous a way that my friend put her arms around him quickly, and held him close. She looked at me over the bright defiant hair and we could not speak.

So we went back into the cold night. It was then that I remembered that the next day would be Christmas Eve.

Always at Christmas the memory of Kevin comes back to me. I am there again in our old church, its stone walls and pillars softened in the candlelight as people throng in to the midnight service. At the back the little model village is displayed on a trestle table. Tiny lights shine out of the windows of the houses, and the pond of frosted glass glistens and sparkles. Bright red paper flowers with silver stalks are lovingly arranged around the table and everyone stops to look and admire. Kevin, with his friends, is sitting very still, his expression rapt. There is a peacefulness about him which I have never seen before, for here he is welcome and wanted.

After all he has come home on this night to his Father's house.

14

Pilgrimage to Lindisfarne

The 750th anniversary of our Church of the Holy Cross at Ryton took place during the second year of Tom's curacy. He was made chairman of the committee which organised the many events to mark the occasion into which the whole community was drawn. These included concerts, madrigals on the rectory lawn, a lively Folk Festival, a Flower Festival, and a visit from our Bishop of Durham who came to preach at Evensong and to meet the people.

The most unforgettable day, which Tom says was, for him, the highlight of his ministry at Ryton, was on a Sunday in the middle of June. Hundreds of people from the six parish churches and four district churches which now serve the ancient parish of Ryton, made a pilgrimage together to Lindisfarne or Holy Island, which lies off the coast of north Northumberland, nearly opposite Bamburgh Castle, which is the site of the ancient home of kings and stands like a massive fortress on the black whinstone outcrop of rock beside the sea. I must digress a little here, for some account of the history of Holy Island, which I have found fascinating, will explain why a pilgrimage to it was so memorable and significant to us, and indeed to all who journey there.

Holy Island was described by Bede, the monk of Jarrow, in his great *History of the English Church and People*, written in the early eighth century; it is a book which is as fascinating and lively to read today in translation as when it was first written. He writes:

"As the tide ebbs and flows, this place is surrounded by sea twice a day like an island, and twice a day the sand dries and joins it to the mainland." From this remote spot, men of marvellous courage came forth in the seventh century to proclaim the Christian faith in Northumbria and far beyond. Their story is part of the rich remembered heritage of this northern land and one which has gripped my imagination for many years. It began with the coming of the saintly Bishop Aidan from Iona at the urgent invitation of the young Christian King Oswald of Northumbria.

Oswald had grown up among the monks on Iona with his sister and brothers, after the slaughter in battle of his father, the Anglo-Saxon King Ethelfrith who ruled from the Humber to the Forth. In 634 A.D. Oswald, who had left Northumbria a young pagan child, returned, now a devoted Christian, to claim his kingdom for Christ. Setting up with his own hands a large wooden cross, not far from the Roman wall near Hexham, he called his army to prayer. After this, a great victory was gained over the heathen King Cadwalla and his much greater forces. The place became known as Heavenfield, and is marked with a cross to this very day.

Aidan, for whom Oswald then sent to convert his people to Christianity, chose Lindisfarne as his See. Possibly it reminded him of Iona. Here a wooden church was built, and simple monastic buildings set up. Aidan initiated the religious life with a band of monks after the Celtic pattern, and he founded a school and spent much time educating and teaching native boys, twelve at first, so that in time they too might become missionaries. Three of the first twelve were later to become bishops, Eata, Cedd and Chad, while many others, including Wilfred of York, were also to be taught by him.

Perhaps it was Aidan's great missionary journeys throughout the length and breadth of the wild country of Northumbria, from Humber to Forth, which bring him alive most vividly to our minds and form one of the most inspiring pictures in English history. For king and bishop travelled great distances together, and while Aidan stopped to preach the gospel wherever there were people to listen, the king would be beside him translating all he said into the language of his people. Believers were baptised, little churches founded, and encouragement and inspiration was given to all who were Christians. Aidan almost always refused to ride a horse, travelling on foot over the rough terrain like the poorest people, for he felt he could meet them better this way, and whenever he met anyone he stopped and spoke to them. Aidan, we are told, was "inspired with a passionate love and goodness, but at the same time was full of a surprising gentleness and moderation", and as Bede tells us, "he never sought or cared for any worldly possessions, and loved to give away to the poor whatever he received from kings and wealthy folk." His whole life was consistent for, as Bede tells us, he lived no other than as he taught.

As we prepared for our pilgrimage, one figure seemed particularly to symbolise our own quest, and to live in our minds in a special way.

Cuthbert was still a young man watching over sheep in the Lammermuir hills, when he saw a vision of angels carrying a great soul to Paradise. A few days later he heard of Aidan's death, and knew then that his vision was an unexpected call to him to serve God too. Cuthbert, said to be a beautiful fair-haired youth, then went to Melrose and became a monk there with the permission of the Abbot, Eata, who had himself been brought up on Lindisfarne by Aidan, and who later was to become Bishop of Lindisfarne and then Hexham. During his years at Melrose, Cuthbert made many missionary journeys from Berwickshire to the Solway and wherever he went people gathered to hear him, for Bede tells us, "he had such a light in his angelic face, and such a love for proclaiming his message" that men everywhere turned to the Christian faith. It was Eata who eventually brought Cuthbert to Lindisfarne "to instruct the brethren", and here he became Prior, and later helped to reconcile the opposing Celtic and Roman factions in the church after the Synod of Whitby in 664, when the decision was made to follow the Roman church's customs and ritual. Largely through him, many believe, it was made possible for the Celtic church of Columba and Aidan, noted for its simplicity but deep piety, to be reconciled with the practices of the church of Augustine and with Rome.

Cuthbert's life as prior was full. Like Aidan he spent years training missionaries on Lindisfarne, crossing to the mainland, and journeying far and wide, teaching, baptising, healing, and celebrating the Mass on a portable altar. Eventually Cuthbert became a hermit at the age of forty-two, having obtained permission to go and live on the uninhabited island of Farne, some miles from Holy Island, so that he might serve God in prayer and solitude; but the monks on Lindisfarne used to row over and visit him, and helped to build him a tiny dwelling and an oratory, and a shelter for those who visited him. His fame as a saintly and holy man spread, and visitors regularly came to see him, rowing across from the mainland. Bede comments that "no one went away without enjoying his consolation, and no one returned accompanied by that sorrow of mind which he had brought thither". It was while he was there that messages and letters came to him telling that he had been unanimously elected as Bishop of Hexham, one of the four bishoprics into which Northumbria had been divided in 684; but he steadfastly refused this honour. At last, Bede tells us, a fleet of boats set out for the little island, "carrying the King (Egfrid) in person, accompanied by the most holy Bishop Trumwine and other devout and distinguished men ... There they were joined by many of the Lindisfarne brethren, and the whole company knelt before him and begged him with tears to consent". At last with sorrow Cuthbert assented, and was consecrated Bishop at York on Easter Day, 685 A.D. He did not, however, go to Hexham. He so much preferred to rule the church of Lindisfarne that it was arranged that the ageing Eata should go to Hexham as

Bishop and Cuthbert should be Bishop of Lindisfarne. Bede describes him at this time as being "afire with heavenly love, unassumingly patient, devoted to unceasing prayer, and kindly to all who came to him for comfort". As a historian Bede had set himself to examine all available records, to secure verbal and written accounts from reliable living authorities, and to give as accurate a history of the English church and people as he could. What we read in his History has, for the most part, the stamp of authenticity. He had personal links with those who had been with the missionaries of Iona and Lindisfarne, and was near enough in time to view them with clarity. In Bede – "Father of English History", as he has been called – "two streams of spiritual influence seemed to meet and blend – the evangelistic passion of the Celtic missionaries, and the disciplined devotion of the Benedictine monks".*

To tread again in the very steps of these early saints whose remarkable story is at the very heart of Northumbria's heritage was for us at Ryton, therefore, a not-to-be-forgotten experience.

A fleet of buses assembled at various points in the area to take us on the two-hour journey north. It was one of those days which nothing seems to mar. From early morning Northumberland lay bathed in brilliant sunshine, and a sense of expectancy filled us all. Shortly after midday we arrived at Beal on the coast, opposite the causeway over which cars and tourists can now reach Holy Island at the hours of low tide. But our purpose was far different. While waiting for the tide to fall, the huge crowd settled in groups on the grass to eat a picnic lunch. We gazed across the miles of sea and empty sands glistening in the sun, and waited. Only at certain hours of the day can one walk across the only safe route over three miles of wet sand, marked at intervals by high posts, leading to the island on the very way the monks travelled to and from the mainland in those far-off days as they set out on their missionary journeys.

*Bishop Hensley Henson of Durham.

There was a movement in the crowd, and at last a number of people went barefoot down to the shore. But at first we found ourselves on slippery seaweed, and then sinking into thick tidal mud which oozed over our feet, and there was a hasty retreat. Like the children of Israel there were those who murmured and almost turned back! Then I saw Tom, far ahead, cassock tucked high into his leather belt at the waist, wade far out to test the depth of a channel of swiftly-flowing water ahead, which barred our way. It came up to his thighs and he seemed likely to disappear for ever before we set out. But the pilgrims were not deterred for long. Soon a better way to the posts was found, and the great concourse of people moved slowly, steadily out onto the wet open sands.

Men and boys carrying high the wooden crosses they had carefully fashioned, took their places at the head of the procession, followed by some of the clergy and the great crowd of pilgrims, and so we set out to Lindisfarne. We walked barefoot in the sunlight, and the great heat was tempered by a light breeze which caressed the face, and our feet were washed by sparkling rivulets of sea water.

As we went on our way, we were all conscious of a surging of the spirit, of happiness and joy. It reminded me of the heady days of the early church. The oldest pilgrim was over eighty, and she walked steadily with the best. The youngest were toddlers, not yet two years old, one pulled in a pushchair, the other perched high on his father's shoulders. Presently the "Hymn of the Church of Northumbria" was started up by those in front, and soon all joined in, taking up the tune, and the voices echoed out across the empty, sunlit sands and drifted back to the shore behind us:

Fishers from the Islands, Shepherds in Strathclyde,
    Clansmen of the Highlands
    Own the Crucified

"From Iona Aidan came to Oswald's home,
    To the heavy laden
    Spake of rest to come."

About a mile out from the shore, with the vast and empty space around us, a lonely figure suddenly and unexpectedly appeared a little way ahead, as if waiting. There fell a sudden hush, a spontaneous silence, and we paused. It was as if he had appeared from nowhere, had perhaps crossed the country to meet us. Tall, bareheaded, barefoot, his long purple cassock vivid against the silver sand, the cross he wore flashing in the sunlight, the Bishop of Jarrow stood there, his hand lightly resting on his tall pastoral shepherd's crook. It was a sublime moment, our rector said later. We were in a strange way caught up in an inexplicable emotion greater than ourselves. It seemed momentarily as if Cuthbert himself stood there, waiting to lead us across, in company with all those who had walked over those sands so long ago.

The Bishop came forward to greet us and, as if with a single united impulse, the procession of people wheeled and turned towards him. Surrounded by all the children, he now led the procession towards the distant island. Without any prompting the crowd began to sing again. It was unrehearsed, magnificent, and the sound rose and fell, and because of the happiness in our hearts the way seemed all too short.

We reached the island two miles further on. Here there was another large gathering of people waiting for us, all those unable to make the journey on foot, the holidaymakers, the vicar and the people of the island, and together we made our way through the streets and past the cluster of houses, on the last stage of our pilgrimage. The Bishop, robed now in mitre and golden and red cope dazzling in the sun, led us inside the ruined walls of the ancient late eleventh-century priory, which, it is thought, may possibly stand on the site of the earliest monastic church. There on the smooth grassy slope, like an amphitheatre, we sang Evensong together, beginning with the triumphant hymn, "Lift high the Cross, the love of Christ proclaim".

The Bishop spoke to us and in that place, still I believe sanctified by the lives of the holy men who lived there long centuries ago, we got a glimpse of all we might do and be in a world that needs the Christian gospel no less urgently now than in those far-off days of the fearless Northumbrian saints of the Celtic church.

After the service we walked on the island, feeling the atmosphere of peace and holiness which slowly fills heart and mind. In the churchyard beside the Priory we gazed at the figure of Aidan holding high a flaming torch. It is carved by an inspired hand. The face looks up, is alive, alight with joy, and there is such a sweetness of expression as causes one to turn away, inexplicably moved.

As I stood there, I thought of the heroic endeavour and unfaltering missionary zeal of those early saints, who had lived and walked and worshipped, prayed and suffered here. I recalled the endless line of men and women called through the long years to go out from Northumbria carrying the gospel of Christ to their world. Persecution and war, poverty and hunger, had not deterred them. In the centuries-long line of those who answered the Call to witness, we of our generation now stood.

It was a privilege, a high honour, I now saw, that Tom was among them, and David too, priested that very month in Southwark Cathedral, and supported by us all as a family. Even the press and media had been curious, fascinated at a father and son ordained almost at the same time in the same family, who had both dedicated their lives to witness for Christ in today's world. There were many of our friends and David's too, who also had heard this Call.

I could not then see what lay ahead. I could not foresee the time of testing that would come when Tom and other men also would be called to "go out", and would have to leave the north, the very place where they belonged and wanted to work, for no living would be found for them in Northumberland or Newcastle; nor how keenly we would feel the parting from home, family, friends and work. I could not know, although I might well have guessed, that we would have to face disappointment, difficulties and sometimes sorrow. But I knew with Tom that it would be death to turn back, death of a commitment and a vision. I could not then have imagined that Tom would be a chaplain in Corfu, and for a short time in Norway; a vicar in a town in Somerset and rector in a village in East Yorkshire. Nor could I have imagined the happiness and joy that would come to us from time to time in our new life. The Holy Spirit still had much to teach us, and we had much to learn.

I did not then know that opportunities would come to me also, of working with many children, and that it would be my task to try and bring them something of Christ's love. Nor that opportunities through writing would be given and I would sometimes have the privilege of speaking on television and radio and trying to witness to my faith. And all this would have been barren and impossible had I not experienced what is meant by the lovely words of the old hymn, and known for myself what it is to be "ransomed, healed, restored, forgiven".

There was something else. We would find that in spite of the church's failings, its burdened structures, its dullness and coldness and in some places its deathly slumber, the hidden flame of faith has not been extinguished. It waits to be fanned into life by those who have opened hearts and minds to Christ's Holy Spirit. For miracles can still happen today. We have seen them. Life *can* pour into the Christian church and into groups of believers, young and old, and they *can* still be given power to witness to Christ, and to work for Him wherever they may be. This we have seen and experienced ourselves. But we are often so dull, so slow, so unsure, so afraid of true emotion, so cold; and the flame flickers feeble and low, and we have nothing to offer to those around us. Yet the world is dying today for Christ's love, and we are called to carry it to others so that through us they may find Him. The task is great, and the Unexpected Call is not to a favoured few. It comes in many forms to all who listen and hear and respond, and in so doing find new life.